The State of Architecture at the Beginning of the 21st Century

The State of Architecture at the Beginning of the 21st Century

Edited by Bernard Tschumi + Irene Cheng

THE MONACELLI PRESS

Columbia Books of Architecture

First published in the United States of America in 2003 by
The Monacelli Press, Inc.
902 Broadway, New York, New York 10010.

Library of Congress Cataloging-in-Publication Data
The state of architecture at the beginning of the 21st century / edited by Bernard Tschumi, Irene Cheng.
p. cm.
Papers presented at the conference held Mar. 28–29, 2003, Columbia Graduate School of Architecture,
Planning, and Preservation in honor of Bernard Tschumi's final year as the dean.
ISBN 1-58093-134-0
1. Architecture, Modern—21st century—Congresses. 2. Architecture—Forecasting—Congresses. I. Tschumi,
Bernard, 1944– . II. Cheng, Irene.
NA687.S73 2003
724'.7—dc22   2003025042

Printed and bound in Canada
Designed by Omnivore, Alice Chung and Karen Hsu

A modified version of the essay by Michael Sorkin appeared in *Architectural Record* in May 2003.

Portions of the essay by Hani Rashid and Lise Anne Couture are drawn from an interview with Michael
Speaks that was published in *A+U* in April 2003.

Contents

What is the state of architecture at the beginning of the twenty-first century? What is the value of asking such an immoderate, overreaching question?

It might be argued that those of us engaged in the practice of architecture today find ourselves in unusually blissful circumstances. Never has the field been more celebrated. Titanium temples of culture and translucent masterpieces appear ubiquitous, while architects have become successful media demigods, busy revitalizing the image of cities in a global economy.

Or is the situation the opposite? In the twenty-first century, will we come to criticize buildings that are famous more for what they look like than for what they do, and architects concerned more with constructing their autobiographies than with developing the art of construction? Will we mourn the death of public space and the disappearance of progressive social programs?

What is the field of architecture today, then, especially as perceived by those at its front lines—architects, architectural writers, and theorists? Historically, architects and artists have often commented on the condition of their discipline, whether through descriptive statements ("this is what is happening"), prescriptive ones ("this is what we must do"), or both. Have the modes of self-analysis and -expression changed? How will a new generation voice itself? These are among the questions we set out to explore in this volume.

Twentieth-century architecture began with a rapid-fire burst of revolutionary declarations. Tracts such as F. T. Marinetti's *Futurist Manifesto* (1909), Le Corbusier's *Towards a New Architecture* (1920), Kasimir Malevich's *Suprematist Manifesto* (1924), and the CIAM "La Sarraz Declaration" (1928) called for significant transformations in architectural practice, including the abandonment of ornament and historical styles, the adoption of new materials and technologies such as mass production, and a reorientation of architectural aims to the needs and problems of industrial society. Many of these statements exhibited features typical of the manifesto form: an impassioned and pithy style, the use of "plain speech," a call for a historical rupture, and a focus on the present, the "now."

By the second half of the twentieth century, the failure of revolutionary dogmas—both in architecture and in global politics—to achieve many of their utopian aims led to a waning of the hortatory impulse in architecture. As Joan Ockman observes in her introduction to *Architecture Culture 1943–1968*, "If the manifesto was the generic expression of the emergent aspirations of the early-twentieth-century avant-gardes, indeed of the period of high modernism itself, its moment was over by the midcentury. An architecture culture largely in retrenchment after the war…was not disposed to such a positive form of enunciation."

At the beginning of the twenty-first century, the question arises: is it worth revisiting the idea of the manifesto in architecture, of a form of declaration that asserts goals and directions for the practice? The intervening influences of poststructuralism and feminism caution against the universal and absolute discourses of earlier manifestos. Few today would have the audacity to proclaim, as the Situationists did in 1960, "To those who do not properly understand us, we say with utter contempt: 'The Situationists, of whom you perhaps believe yourselves to be the judges, will one day judge you.'" A declaration in today's "postcritical" and self-conscious age might be closer in spirit to Tristan Tzara's *Dada Manifesto* (1918), in which the author stated: "I write a manifesto and I want nothing, yet I say certain things, and in principle, I am against manifestoes, as I am also against principles…"

The essays in this volume do not claim to be manifestos as such, and yet many perform a comparable role, taking stock of the present or laying out possible strategies for the future. Some are more manifesto-like than others, whether through their exhortatory tone, their emphasis on the present as a moment of change and transition, or their anticipation of unrealized futures. Others take a more critical, tentative, inquisitive, or even pessimistic perspective on the state of architecture at the beginning of the twenty-first century. A few devote as much space to images as to text, on the premise that pictures—and works of architecture themselves—can make a statement as powerfully as words can. All of the essays follow the manifesto's convention of conciseness, and therefore tend toward the epigrammatic rather than the expository, the sketchlike as opposed to the fully rendered.

These essays present a range of views from sixty of the world's leading architectural designers, historians, theorists, and critics who gathered for a conference at Columbia University on March 28 and 29, 2003. Also included are texts originating from two keynote lectures that were delivered prior to the conference. The list of participants is by no means fully representative of the diversity of current architectural thinking and practice. With a few exceptions, conference moderators and respondents came from the faculty of Columbia's Graduate School of Architecture, Planning and Preservation, while panelists were invited from outside the school. The conference structure has been roughly preserved in this book: each section begins with a short introduction, followed by an essay that originated as a moderator's statement, articles by panelists, and shorter respondents' statements.

The conference participants were grouped into eight sections, or themes, each combining two basic categories of architectural discourse and practice. The idea was to juxtapose concepts that are not typically thought of together — politics and material, or globalization and criticism, for instance — to see what new formulations might arise.

More generally, both the conference and this book are intended as forums for a kind of collective stocktaking, an opportunity for architects to gather, pause, and reflect on current and future aims. The conference took place against the backdrop of a major event in recent American history: the start of the United States war on Iraq, which some saw as extending from the events of September 11, 2001. The attacks on the Pentagon and the World Trade Center in particular highlighted the global importance of architecture as both symbol and shelter. Those events perhaps have compelled architects to find something to say once again, and to say it with the directness and vigor that marked the declarations of the last century.

Bernard Tschumi and Irene Cheng

The design of avant-garde works of architecture, influenced by science fiction and digital and aerospace technologies, strains ever toward the future. At the same time, the popular idea of the beautiful city is based on nineteenth-century or even medieval stereotypes. How do we explain this contradiction in aesthetics?

Indeed, the criteria of aesthetics seem inappropriate for evaluating contemporary urban areas, which today are the breeding grounds and blister points for myriad social problems and dynamics. Modern cities include many elements—infrastructure, encounters with cultural difference, sprawl, and economic centralization—but aesthetic pleasure seems too subjective and idiosyncratic to be a guiding principle for urban planning. What then is the relationship between aesthetics and urbanism? What can architects offer the city? And what might an avant-garde urbanism be in the twenty-first century?

Kenneth Frampton begins by reflecting on the dystopian landscape of New York City's outer boroughs and questions whether the city of the twenty-first century will be fundamentally different, or whether it will simply reconfront the unresolved environmental, social, and economic problems of the twentieth century.

Looking to the future, Winy Maas argues that architects can reassert themselves in public debates about cities by analyzing key global trends, developing new strategies, and creating tools and languages to communicate their ideas more effectively. Stan Allen and James Corner offer an example of architects creating novel tools and languages. They abandon the traditional modernist bias toward urban density and instead use the term *field urbanism* to describe their approach to addressing the new, horizontal structure of many contemporary cities.

A very different strategy is adopted by Wolf Prix, who discusses his recent shift from a preoccupation with the formal properties of objects to an interest in the possibility of creating public space through architecture. Form, Prix implies, can generate urbanism rather than merely supplant it.

Probably no one would disagree with Prix more than Robert A. M. Stern, the master planner of the redesigned Times Square. Forget about the forms, he admonishes architects, and instead, look for the vision of the good society that architecture should promote. Michael Sorkin shares Stern's interest in finding a vision for the good city but, unlike Stern, believes that the architectural avant-garde's "quiver of innovation and transgression" might yet offer solutions to the dilemmas faced by cities—and citizens—of an unbalanced world.

Finally, Gregg Pasquarelli succinctly frames the tension between today's cult of architectural objects and its politically docile forms of urban planning. Between these two poles, he asks, are there possibilities for creating works of urban architecture that are both progressive and beautiful?

Kenneth Frampton

Brief Reflections on the Predicament of Urbanism

A recent publication by the artists Laurent Malone and Dennis Adams recorded in photographic form the random topographic panorama that unfolded as they took a walk in a straight line from a storefront in Manhattan to the initial threshold of Kennedy Airport.

A more unaesthetic and strangely repetitive urban fabric—apart from the monumental tranquility of the occasional cemetery—would be hard to imagine. It is a dystopia from which we are usually shielded by the kaleidoscopic blur of the average taxi window, which more often than not is only partially transparent. Looked at through the pedestrian optic of Malone and Adams, this is in-your-face urban fabric. It is an oddly paranoid, rather ruthless, instrumental, and resentful landscape compounded by endless chain-link fences, graffiti, razor wire, rusted ironwork, overheated fast food, signs of all kinds, housing projects that are barely distinguishable from penal institutions, the occasional fading ad or former cinema about to turn into a bingo hall, and as one gets farther out on the island, the would-be colonial fantasy of closely packed parsimonious suburban houses with their white plastic siding. And everywhere, of course, the indifferent signs of hardscrabble economic survival about to get harder, and the ubiquitous and indispensable automobile. One cannot help asking oneself if these are truly the phantasmagoric but unbearably tedious shades of the American dream for which we are ostensibly liberating the Middle East.

Is this once again a picture of an environmental balance sheet that hasn't changed much in forty years? Just more of the same and hence just as predictable? Is there some fatal, inescapable paralysis that prevails, separating the increasingly smart, technological extravagance of our armaments from the widespread dumbness and meanness of our environment? A recent report issued by the British government states that 90 percent of what will exist twenty years from now has already been built. Thus aesthetics and urbanism in the twenty-first century bring one back to all the unanswerable questions of the previous century.

Dennis Adams and Laurent Malone, *JFK*, 2002

Winy Maas

TOWARD AN URBANISTIC ARCHITECTURE

More than ever the world has become a battlefield for urban planning, and more than ever a coherent urbanistic approach is lacking. In a world where collective efforts are countered or even replaced by individualism, where politics are uncertain and the swings of unpredictable economies discourage communal investments, overall planning has become an activity for hobbyists, a dress code for politicians, and a last resort for stuck idealists. Amid these shifting certainties, urbanism has become a haven for resistance and protectionism, a question of creating zones rather than possibilities. Any new development these days seems to be connected with this protectionism. In such times, even New Urbanism has become an anachronism. Few architects want to speak about cities anymore. In a time when the culture of objects is ascendant, what architect wants to be an urbanist?

Nevertheless, many questions remain. What should the city be in the future? How can it overcome the deconcentration tendencies we see in New Jersey and suburban New York? What programs should the city contain? What infrastructural issues need to be addressed?

The crisis in urbanism goes hand in hand with a converging tendency in architecture. The notion that from a technical standpoint everything can be constructed coincides with the awareness that every type of architectural object has already been made. Have we reached the limits of architecture?

In the competition for the World Trade Center site, many architects from different backgrounds and rival camps, including my firm, **MVRDV**, came up with similar themes: towers that branch, kiss, split, and hover, all aspiring for urban life higher up. They all embraced increasing densities, growth, and a future planet inhabited by more people. Blob and data designers fused with rationalists and super-modernists in an almost communal enterprise. This seeming unification challenges the convention that architects act like Houdinis—ever elusive and uneasy with a fixed position, engaging in behaviors that border on escapism and avoidance of responsibility.

Economic and political crises reduce the possibilities for experimental architecture. Moreover, the rapid spread of ideas through international magazines, the increasing opportunities for collab-

orating with local architects abroad, the speed of technology, and the employment of a common pool of students lead to a convergence rather than to a differentiation of architectures. In the coming era, the classic, artistically oriented role for architecture must be preserved as originality and authenticity are increasingly challenged.

At this moment, when urbanism has lost its allure and architecture encounters its limits, to what should a new generation dedicate itself? Research has become the fashionable means to address the uncertainty of the current situation. This is a helpful step as long as it is combined with constructive proposals. Research can uncover possible agendas for the design of future cities and landscapes—new programs, configurations, and architectures that might offer an escape from the current crisis. Currently, the world is dominated by cheap, banal structures, a sea in which the architectural object ceases to exist. This bifurcates the role of architecture. On the one hand, the interior becomes more important, and on the other, urbanism is brought to the fore. Time (temporality, flexibility, changeability), scale, and infrastructure become major themes.

Does this open the way for a wider agenda for architects? Can architects aspire to take on larger issues and thus be idealistic again? Shouldn't architects take positions, maybe even outside our own domain, instead of being only critical and cynical? I would like to suggest a few of the large-scale sociological and ecological processes that will shape architectural practice in the decades to come, and in which architects might intervene.

GROWTH

The growth of the world population will lead to a tremendous demand for space, not only for buildings but also for farmland and areas reserved for nature. How can we accommodate these demands? Can we do it through sprawl or should we densify? Can we densify not only our cities but also our zones of industrial production? Can this then lead to new synergies? Can we make it attractive for suburbanites to live more densely? Can we create new typologies of density?

MIGRATION

In a world of stark economic differentials, migration will be a crucial phenomenon. If we were to distribute the world population evenly based on today's data, the United States would have to house four times its current population. The population of the Netherlands would triple. A quarter of the migrants would come from India. This may suggest new kinds of urbanism and architecture, such as structures that accommodate housing and offices in shifts. Flexibility will be important. The neutral plan may appear again. We will need to invent a lighter approach to urbanism that allows us to easily change large parts of our environment, turning cities back into agricultural or natural areas.

MOBILITY

In order to accommodate these changes, we need to forge strong connections between architecture and infrastructure. Traffic nodes and smart programmatic combinations will speed the pace of global transformations.

SPECIALIZATION

In a world where boundaries are being revised, regions or urban clusters will become more important. Competition between regions may lead to more specialization, which will, in turn, lead to economic concentration and accumulation of knowledge. Specialization encourages trade and causes interdependence between clusters, creating a more stable world. Specialization of cities will lead to new programs and architectures, and will affect the composition of the cities involved as they adapt to a more global agenda.

CLIMATE

Climate changes will generate new landscapes. Some zones will be drier, others wetter. Architecture will have to accommodate these new conditions.

Architecture should be at the center of the public debates on space once again. Space can be a vehicle for accommodating political, economic, and societal demands, and for realizing solutions. Architecture can provide perspective. The methods for doing so can be extremely varied and rich, ranging from the creation of beautiful objects that assuage daily life to apocalyptic proposals that clamor for a reaction. More than in the past, architecture has the potential to occupy a wide range of communicative possibilities and to utilize various means, media, and scales. It can range from global spatial studies and visualizations (as in our study on the migration city) to specific studies that criticize current tendencies and put forward alternatives (as in our Pig City project) to the creation of icons that communicate with a wider audience, outside of architecture (as in our Dutch Pavilion). It can also explore in-depth tools for communication, such as our Functionmixer and Regionmaker—software programs that allow one to enter certain parameters in order to optimize a given programmatic or urban condition.

Architecture can be a tool for communication. It therefore needs to develop languages that will allow it to converse with other domains or professions and to convince clients who might not be interested in broader agendas.

Criticism must have a stronger role as well. We have to judge aims against results. If so-called silent or minimalist architecture in Switzerland exacerbates the withdrawn tendencies of the region, for instance, is this a good strategy for Switzerland? As the influence of polemical architecture in the Netherlands wanes in the current political climate, does it become counterproductive?

Today, architecture is moving toward the development of "devices" that can combine large-scale issues with individualized input, and analysis with proposals. Architecture in the future will be consumer oriented, connecting bottom-up with top-down. It will come to be seen as an instrument for general observation, as a messenger for urban transactions, and as a communicator of wider processes. Maybe architecture can then overcome Ulrich Beck's notion that "individualism, diversity, and skepticism are rooted in Western culture." Maybe then we can become more active, assertive, communicative, and in the end, productive, in shaping the future city.

URBAN NATURES

Stan Allen/James Corner

Aesthetics + Urbanism

FIELD URBANISM

In the late twentieth century, transportation, flexible capital accumulation, and the suburban ideal of private housing have led to the emergence of a radically horizontal, field-like urbanism. A new city form has developed, extended in the horizontal dimension but marked by points of intensity and exchange—nodes where the local thickening of section produces three-dimensional effects within the shallow depth of the contemporary city.

As a consequence, the difference between city, country, and suburb is fast disappearing: in 1979, 85 percent of the office space in the United States was located in cities; today office construction is divided equally between the suburbs and the city. Greater Phoenix is anticipated to have ten million inhabitants by 2004; considered as a region, metropolitan Los Angeles is actually denser than New York. The new city is founded on mobility and is porous to the natural landscape. Such "sprinkler cities" are often knowledge-driven and arise independent of older hubs. Moreover, the social character of the suburban landscape is changing: a majority of Asian Americans, 50 percent of Hispanic Americans, and 40 percent of African Americans live in suburbs. There is nothing monolithic or objectlike about this emergent horizontal field. Rather than existing in search of some kind of organizing body, these new city forms are an amalgam of mobile agents, provisional colonies, and diverse components. They are composed of small units and collectives rather than singularities, and bottom-up organizations rather than top-down orders.

In response to the dynamic complexity of contemporary urbanism, Field Operations, our office, has deployed numerous organizing strategies to develop landscape and ecological approaches to urbanism.

Ecology and landscape are useful because, unlike the architectural object, they escape definitive control or closure; instead, they address the complexity of loosely structured organizations that grow and change with time. Today, landscape architects are embracing change and designing landscapes that anticipate a succession of states: a fluctuating choreography of speciation, shifting spatial characteristics, and new uses over time. These changes are not merely quantitative—the result of, for example, plants growing into maturity—but qualitative. Working with a precise spatial framework, our projects aim to create the conditions under which distinct—sometimes unanticipated—spatial characteristics may emerge. We recognize that urbanism cannot be designed and controlled as a totality but instead must be projected, steered, and actively managed to grow and change over time. In this sense, cities and landscapes are diagrams subjected to a limited deregulation; they are more the product of cultivation and management than of design per se. In developing the strategies for this new landscape urbanism, a working vocabulary begins to emerge:

topography	field
surface	cluster
mat	strata
blanket	flow
network	feeder
pathway	thread
matrix	diagram
emergent	map
infrastructure	sprawl

NEW NATURES

The radical claim of the 1980s was for extending architecture and urbanism into the territory of landscape—in other words, promoting culture over nature and making landscape artificial. More recently, a new information-based model of nature has emerged and, with it, a notion of landscape as synthetic nature.

At a time when the line between artificial and natural is increasingly blurred by developments in genetic engineering and changing biological paradigms, it is possible to rethink the strict division of natural and artificial in landscape. For us, the nature/culture and artificial/natural distinctions are no longer interesting. To say "all nature is constructed" has no critical force; it is simply a given, a starting point for a more complex synthesis. Synthetic landscapes make use of the logics of natural systems and the dynamics of ecological feedback without the romantic attachment to a pastoral idea of nature. When nature is wholly synthetic, it is already disengaged from any pastoral idea of nature or its corollary, the poetics of dereliction or the industrial picturesque. It doesn't need steel trees or plastic turf to announce its artificiality. Like the city, these synthetic landscapes are active rather than passive; design has a transformative, activating agency. Natural operations are used to produce artificial, ambient effects. Instead of nature as a scenic, benign force, we are proposing a new metabolism—the synthetic landscape as a bacterial machine. Here, innovative landscape-based urban practices draw from geography, politics, ecology, architecture, and engineering in working toward the production of new urban natures.

From top: Metropolitan plasma; field urbanism; surfaces; bacterial urbanism

b5 2 c6: Public Space

The gradual privatization of urban public space in Western cities is having profound effects on contemporary architecture as a whole. Faced with a lack of public funds, cities and local authorities are increasingly unable to play an active role in urban planning and instead acquiesce to private investors who help themselves to the biggest and best pieces of the city. It is a game whose end is easily predicted: architecture will end up as infrastructure built to maximize profits within the global economy.

Architecture can resist this instrumentalization by becoming an agent of a new philosophy of urban planning. Conversely, without architecture, urban planning may soon cease to exist. The master plan is dead. Today, the gridded and idealized urban space of the nineteenth century exists only on paper, superseded long ago by the actual dynamics of urban transformations. Contemporary urban interventions take place in an amorphous and imponderable space, analogous to chess figures moving horizontally across blurred television screens—but the grid of the chessboard has disappeared, as have the rules determining how the pieces move. Yet the figures remain: a rook is still a rook, and its moves are still significant, even though the coordinates of this movement can no longer be plotted within an abstract frame of reference (B5 to C6, for example).

The more the background recedes, however, the more distinct the figures can become; in the wake of the implosion of the old order, it is these figures that make a city. Their coming together creates force fields of tension and new, dynamic urban spaces. This process is infinitely more complex than laying down a grid and filling it up square by square with architecture. Space is no longer predetermined but rather develops through the tensions and interrelationships between figures. This is the basis for a vigorous new model of urbanism.

This agenda has shaped the recent work of Coop Himmelb(l)au. The UFA Cinema Center (1993–98) in Dresden, Germany, is the first of several projects that attempt to create public space through architecture. The model of the building as object is replaced by the idea of an urban transistor—an architecture that is capable of amplifying the urban spaces adjoining it through its own transistorlike spatial organization. The most important aspect of the UFA Cinema Center is not its function as a movie theater but its urban qualities. In addition to creating a spacious lobby and a roofed-in space for showing films, we raised the theater box to allow a public passageway to connect two key city spaces below. Inside, a vertically ascending spatial sequence—best described as Piranesi meets MTV—unfolds, abandoning once and for all the idea of a centrally perceived spatial perspective.

For us, the UFA Cinema Center represents a new paradigm of spatial definition and formal design based on two interconnected ideas: the free configuration of three-dimensional figures (similar to the chess figures on the blank screen) and an overarching cover that unites them. In successive projects, we developed this paradigm further, particularly in our project for an urban entertainment center in Guadalajara, Mexico.

In order to organize the complex program of this last project, which includes sixteen cinemas, a shopping mall, restaurants, bars, entertainment, and a media center, we broke up the main body of the building to an even greater extent than in Dresden. The envelope is opened up, revealing a landscape of sculptural volumes distributed inside. Here, the cinemas—which in Dresden were still incorporated into the cement block—are liberated and serve as individual, space-forming elements. While the public space of the lobby in Dresden is still surrounded sculpturally by the body of the crystal, in Guadalajara the space-cover is a planar roof that floats over the ground like a flying carpet. Unlike the traditional urban typology of public squares and piazzas, where the facades of the surrounding buildings serve to define the space, at Guadalajara, the street walls are rotated ninety degrees to form two horizontal planes: a bottom level located eleven meters below grade and the flying carpet floating above. The empty space sandwiched between the two levels is the urban environment. The sides are left open to allow it to interact with its surroundings like a transistor, and the space inside is animated by the constant flow of movement through it. Spatial sculptures mark critical points where the flows are arrested, redirected, and intensified. Breaking up the architectural object to create a spatially differentiated eventscape makes it possible to transcend the common clichés associated with the shopping mall and the urban entertainment center. Anchor stores are no longer needed to support the less attractive programs as they are in Victor Gruen's classic concept of the shopping mall. Rather, the project as a whole is more like a buzzing beehive of activity, in which a number of local points of attraction combine to form a vibrating field of energy.

UFA Cinema Center, Dresden, Germany, 1993–98

Robert A. M. Stern

URBAN-ISM IS ABOUT HUMAN LIFE

Architecture is not an avant-garde; it is not an art movement. Architecture is about the here and now. It is, as Winy Maas implies, an instrumentality. But it is not an instrumentality with a grand set of plans—at least not physical plans like Daniel Burnham or Le Corbusier would have proposed in the early part of the twentieth century. As an architect and educator, I am interested in the tension between the global and local. Between the two, I come down for the local. It has been said that all politics is local politics. All planning is local planning. All architecture is one building next to another building; that is, if we're going to have coherent cities or places, I'm nervous about the bold, global intervention.

I think it's a time for the healing gesture—and I'm not referring specifically to the war with Iraq or even to the World Trade Center site, although they are certainly both significant places that require healing. I'm thinking of the entire landscape that we have left behind us in the Western world—the result of changing patterns of industrialization and settlement. One can take the train from New York City to Boston and see miles and miles of land waiting to find a new use—industrial land that could become new urban neighborhoods or parks or maybe something in between. That is an urgent challenge for us. We don't need new cities; we need to reuse and make better use of our existing urban areas. We don't need to take new land; we need to reclaim wasted, abandoned land.

There are encouraging signs, though they're not generally spoken about in the architectural academy. Large swaths of the South Bronx have been rebuilt, even if they are not architecturally distinguished. But in the Bronx, the city and its streets have been recaptured for people, buildings have been erected in which people can live with reasonable dignity, shops are coming back to life. Maybe every site does not call for an architectural art project.

The South Bronx and places like it—and not so-called junk space—are the battlegrounds and fields of the future. The idea of junk space has been articulated recently in magazines. Yes, we have junk space, but we don't need architects to theorize it. Just because it's there doesn't mean we have to love it. Instead, we should understand it and then look back again at its opposite: compact urbanism.

We need to think more about how people live. At the risk of sounding like a sentimental sociologist, this is where architects should aim their energy. Architects need to get out of the narrow confines of ideology and into the fresh air of the real world a great deal more than most of them do.

Urbanism is about human life. It is not about human form. It is not about art movements. Architecture is an experiential art in which all the circumstances of knowledge and technique are brought together to create the possibility of memorable and unexpected encounters occurring on street corners and sidewalks. That is the heart of the issue. We must make and preserve these cities, and for that, we need a vision of the good. What is a good city? What is the good life that we as architects should advocate? We should answer these questions rather than compete to leave our mark on the city through form.

Michael Sorkin

THE AVANT-GARDE IN TIME OF WAR

Like their civilian counterparts, military planners are experts at zoning. After the first night of "shock and awe" in Iraq on March 20, 2003, Americans were introduced to a neighborhood of evil, a continuous concentration of the architecture of the Saddamite regime, an area of darkness, precisely red-lined to become a pyrotechnic cauldron, ready for its close-up from the roof of the Al-Rashid or Palestine Hotels. Dots on the map suggested that we administered the appropriate corrective dose only where it was needed. By pathologizing in advance all that we hit, the noisome problem of collateral damage was obviated: it's just urban renewal. Indeed, according to an op-ed piece by Daryl G. Press in the March 26, 2003, *New York Times*, Baghdad was particularly well designed for invasion. Lacking tall buildings and laced—unlike Grozny or Mogadishu—with broad boulevards, the city's terrain was not, as Press wrote laconically, "ideal for urban defense."

There was something striking in the coincidence of the planning endgame at Ground Zero with the violent site clearing and promised reconstruction in Iraq. Even before the end of the war, the *Times* reported that the administration had invited Bechtel, Fluor, Halliburton, Parsons, Washington (successor to Morrison-Knudson), and the Berger Group to bid on billions of dollars in projects via an accelerated process. "Bechtel would be proud to rebuild Iraq," a spokesman was quoted as saying, and surely they would be proud to get a piece of the action in downtown New York City as well. Iraq would require its own development corporation, and the administration suggested that these contracts would be supervised by an "interim authority" (shades of the Lower Manhattan Development Corporation and the Port Authority), only answerable upward. War becomes the extension of planning by other means.

Our own response as architects has been uninspiring. Architecture's political voice speaks many tongues, and there is no reason to assume that our views—never mind our styles of expression—should be uniform. To the contrary, liberty (and its product, difference) is the repudiation of the single voice. At the same time, this expressive latitude does not mean a world of endless relativism, in which the defense of principle is made moot by an idea of tolerance that reduces social relations to a Hobbesian jungle of pure opportunism and anything goes. In particular, we look to our avant-garde for a riposte to power, for our own targets of opportunity. Avant-gardes always harbor the political in the idea of the overthrow of the status quo. To escape mere nihilism, though, there must be some integral vision of the good, however obscure its forms at present. Unfortunately, our response to the destruction of the idea of the city by neoliberal globalization or by neocolonial warfare has produced little constructive speculation about urbanism's future. Having seen the looming disaster, too many of our most talented have simply embraced it: too many architects are becoming proponents of sprawl and the one-size-fits-all mentality that is strangling the earth.

But what ideas of the good city are truly worth defending? And how can the architectural avant-garde use its quiver of innovation and transgression to defend them? For me, the city confronts four major challenges in realizing its future, all of which have implications for form. The first of these is sustainability, the idea that numbers and resources must be balanced in order to conserve and enhance the health of both cities and the planet. The second issue is access. This entails both the just distribution of global resources and the freedom of the city that is a fundamental right of urban citizenship. The third is the defense of privacy from the multiplication of techniques of surveillance and manipulation that prevent us from freely forming and maintaining our sense of self. Finally, valuable living cultural and physical ecologies must be preserved. No intelligent form of urbanism can neglect the defense of its historic successes.

On an exponentially urbanizing planet, the construction of new and sustainable cities is an urgent necessity, and we haven't risen to the challenge. Given the struggle between the goals I've listed and the pressures of a winnowing globalization and militarization of culture, the challenge lies both in how to build these cities and how to find the means for expressing their individuality. Neither nostalgic visions nor the depredations of planning via the ineffable wisdom of the market will do: not only bombs obliterate. This assault puts a premium on artistic invention, on the creation of singular architectures that are sustainable, malleable, and beautiful. And it is here that an engaged avant-garde becomes more crucial than ever.

If the avant-garde is to have a utility beyond indulgence, it's time for both excess and straight talking, for the surrender of irony and hair-splitting intelligence to a frenzy of demands for a better world. The strategy of the avant-garde always depends on too much, on some willing form of bad behavior, on blurring old certainties. But totalitarianism trumps ambiguities every time. War is the ultimate bad behavior, and the canny politicians in charge of the carnage in Iraq—by constantly presenting *themselves* as an avant-garde (inventors of the "revolution in military affairs" and pioneers of a new "battlespace")—try to supersede their own savagery by giving it fresh form. We must do better than this. What's needed now are clear propositions at the scale of globalizers, whole cities imagined from scratch, big chunks of alternative realities. Against the aesthetics of alienation and annihilation we must respond with fresh forms of survival and joy. Architecture must take the field.

ARCHITECTURE BEYOND FORM

Gregg Pasquarelli

Today, many architects who are interested in shaping cities as well as buildings face a contradiction: on the one hand, planned urbanism simply materializes the existing political apparatus, while on the other, architecture tends toward the market-driven production of fashion objects, removed from wider urban and social concerns. If formalism does not lead to invention, then how does the next generation of architects begin to think about a new kind of operative architectural or urban design practice that leads us closer to the goal of promoting human life over form?

Instead of traditional top-down planning practices, I suggest that architects might look for specific, localized opportunities to intervene in the city's fabric and infrastructure. Instead of being guided by a concern for the purely functional or purely formal, we need to investigate processes—not only the processes involved in construction but also processes of design and use.

Our office, SHoP, recently designed a pedestrian bridge to span Rector Street in New York City. The first piece of infrastructure to be built in lower Manhattan after September 11, 2001, the bridge was the end result of an intense process of negotiation between many parties: the Battery Park City Authority, the New York State Department of Transportation, commuters, and local residents. The use of a prefabricated box-truss system allowed this unique structure to be built quickly and efficiently. The facade, composed of two sizes of panel that are varied in position and spacing, affords diverse views and the circulation of light and air. A temporary structure that addresses an immediate need, the bridge is simultaneously both infrastructure and an object of design, without being reducible to either.

Politics + Material

Even the untrained observer knows that wood, concrete, glass, steel, and plastic communicate specific feelings or values—warmth, oppression, openness, and disposability, for instance. But how are the meanings of materials determined? Are they innate or acquired? Can these effects be analyzed, harnessed, and deployed to achieve more than simply setting an atmosphere or mood? Is it possible to provoke through materials?

Certainly, we can find examples of the politicization of materials in recent architecture. When the renovated Reichstag building opened in 1999, many critics hailed the building's new glass dome as a symbol of the transparency of democracy. Others questioned whether the appearance of openness could be equated with the condition of governmental accessibility or honesty. The Reichstag shows that while materials undoubtedly carry meanings—cultural, social, and economic—wielding these significations is not a simple task.

Steven Holl suggests that the incertitude of material meanings, far from being a liability, is one of architecture's most powerful tools. The phenomenal experience of architecture cannot be reduced to a single interpretation. Holl suggests that the potential of materials lies in their power to evoke rather than to dictate meaning. Detlef Mertins provides a cautionary historical perspective on how modern architects tried to link material to progressive politics. Recounting the attempts by designers in the 1950s to associate the new materials of glass, steel, and aluminum with democracy and a utopian modernity, Mertins provides insights into why architects today might shy away from such sweeping claims.

An example of an innovative contemporary material practice is found in the work of Toshiko Mori, who documents how an ancient technology—weaving—is currently being put to radical new uses. Since recent advances in material technologies have tended to come from fields outside of architecture, she suggests that architects adopt a "scavenger mentality" in exploring and utilizing new materials. A different approach is illustrated in the work of Wiel Arets, who demonstrates the power of materials to integrate disparate elements into a lucid whole, using the example of an art gallery he designed in the Netherlands.

Jesse Reiser and Nanako Umemoto argue for a wider conception of the term *materials,* defining architecture as the organization of matter in space. They use diagrams to uncover the intelligence embedded in the material world and to translate it into architectural interventions.

Examining an important recent development in architecture, Victoria Meyers looks at the rise of "green" materials, arguing that this moniker cannot be used merely as a billboard for environmental concern but should reflect a deeper attention to architecture's connection with its ecology. Finally, Evan Douglis provides a sobering meditation on the power of politics to make—and unmake—the material world.

Steven Holl

IDEA, PHENOMENON, AND MATERIAL

There is a story that when Louis Sullivan lay on his deathbed in a little hotel room, someone rushed in and said, "Mr. Sullivan, your Troescher Building is being torn down." Sullivan raised himself up and responded, "If you live long enough, you'll see all your buildings destroyed. After all, it's only the idea that counts."

It is the idea that counts. The concept, whether an explicit statement or a subjective demonstration, establishes an order, a field of inquiry, and a limited principle. An organizing idea is a hidden thread connecting disparate parts. An architecture based on a limited concept begins with dissimilarity and variation but ends up illuminating the singularity of a specific situation. In this way, concept can be more than an idea driving a design; it can establish a miniature utopian focus.

The essence of a work of architecture is the organic link between idea and phenomenal experience that develops when a building is realized. Architecture begins with a metaphysical skeleton of time, light, space, and matter in an unordered state; modes of composition are open. Through line, plane, and volume, culture and program are given an order, an idea, and perhaps a form. Materials—the transparency of a membrane, the chalky dullness of a wall, the glossy reflection of opaque glass—intermesh in reciprocal relationships that form the particular experience of a place. Materials interlock with the senses to move the perceiver beyond acute sight to tactility. From linearity, concavity, and transparency to hardness, elasticity, and dampness, the haptic realm opens. Through making, we realize that an idea is a seed to be grown into phenomena. The hope is to unite intellect with feeling, and precision with soul.

Architecture must remain experimental and open to new ideas and aspirations in the face of conservative forces that constantly push it toward the already proven, already built, and already thought. Architects must explore the not yet felt. The realization of one inspired idea in turn inspires others. Phenomenal experience is worth the struggle. It yields a silent response—the joy radiated in the light, space, and materials of architecture.

My favorite material is light. Without light, space remains in oblivion. Light's myriad sources, its conditions of shadow and shade, and its opacity, transparency, translucency, reflection, and refraction intertwine to define or redefine space. Light makes space uncertain. What a pool of yellow light does to a simple volume, or what a paraboloid of shadow does to a bone-white wall—these comprise the transcendental realm of the phenomena of architecture.

I recently had an opportunity to make something out of just light and one other material, frozen water. The work is a nine-meter cube that I created in collaboration with the sculptor Jene Highstein. One enters the cube and comes into a space of reflection. The idea is that this architectural space is made of almost nothing. A month after its completion, it disappears and leaves no trace. Using materials as minimal and ethereal as light and water, one can make something that expresses an idea.

The design for the cube was based on a historical event in the city of Rovaniemi in northern Finland. At the end of World War II, the Germans burned down the entire city as they retreated. They didn't have to do it—the war was nearly over. When the inner circle of the nine-meter cube melts through, the first view one has is directed precisely toward Rovaniemi.

Between idea and phenomenon, meanings vibrate, gather, loosen, disperse, shine, and mutate. Even delayed meanings may exert pressure, crack, fissure, and be pulverized.

Steven Holl and Jene Highstein, *Oblong Voidspace*, Rovaniemi, Finland, 2002

Detlef Mertins

NOW AND THEN

Linking construction materials and politics, especially the politics of progressive or revolutionary change, has been a recurring impulse of modern architects in the twentieth century. The new materials of glass, steel, and concrete were expected to manifest a new society. These artificial, synthetic materials lent themselves particularly well to industrialized modes of production—standardization and serial fabrication—and therefore they could accommodate a new society at a mass scale. For reformers, revolutionaries and conservatives alike, this gave the new materials a political charge. The emergence of a new, potentially utopian era was thought to be just around the corner, contingent only on realizing the possibilities of a material medium whose spatio-structural logic would distinguish the modern from previous historical eras. In this way, the politics of modern materials rested on their essentialization and historicization.

Consider two examples from America in the 1950s. Konrad Wachsmann's aircraft hangar for the U.S. Air Force (1959) was an exuberant cantilevering space frame made of lightweight tubular aluminum with vertical supports set 120 feet apart. Structural enthusiasts of this period believed that peace, harmony, and democracy could be achieved by harnessing the scientific laws of nature. The science of materials, physics, and engineering was thus linked to radical politics, as was architecture like Louis Kahn and Anne Tyng's proposal for Philadelphia's City Hall (1953), a high-rise space frame with a ground plane that was open both literally and symbolically.

As Sarah Goldhagen has pointed out, such claims relied on analogies—between biology and engineering, between natural organisms and human structures—that proliferated in architectural circles during the postwar period. The cover of the spring 1953 issue of the student journal from the School of Design of the North Carolina State College featured microscopic organisms, known as radiolarians, first discovered and published by the zoologist Ernst Haeckel in the 1870s. Haeckel sug-

gested that art and design might learn from the capacity of these organisms to produce an infinite variety of beautiful forms. The radiolarians were composed of the most simple and primitive of all elements; this was seen as the key to their multiplicity. They were found all over the world and were able to adapt to different climates and milieus. In this respect they became exemplary for a conception of morphogenesis that combined sameness and difference, universality and heterogeneity.

Ludwig Mies van der Rohe was also interested in science and technology, but he did not consider technology to be capable of delivering utopia. While he too believed in the role of historical forces to ultimately usher in a new world, he saw his task as bringing the industrial era of modernity to a close by resolving its most characteristic building types into "clear constructions." This required "battles of spirit" whose techniques of clarification included elemental articulation, geometry, proportion, spatial fluidity, and surface treatment. Rather than naturalizing technology, he mathematized it. While the structure of his immense project for the convention hall in Chicago (1953–54) appears to be a space frame, it is in fact a two-way spanning structure made with fourteen-inch steel I-beams. He chose the I-beam because he considered it to be the most characteristic structural element of the age, not the lightest or most efficient. Welded into a geometric figure, the beams produced a weighty image of a grid—the iron grid of modernity transformed into a symbol of cosmos and democracy latent within the chaos of modern times.

In retrospect, the political claims of both examples—one invoking the authority of biology, the other of geometry—appear naive in their essentialism and historicization. Science itself is not a stable authority but is always developing new models to account for things not previously understood. Utopia did not emerge through biotechnics, although numerous remarkable works certainly came under its aegis. Nor was modernity fulfilled in clear constructions, as Mies had hoped, thereby bringing the industrial era to a close and opening the way for a new stage in history.

There are many continuities between then and now. We live precisely in the next stage of the history of modernization, in a new technological era. Yet it is important to note the differences. Although certain modernist and avant-garde tropes are being reiterated, including the dream that new technologies will lead to an open and dynamic spatiality and greater freedom, claims for architecture today are decidedly limited. While programs of social responsibility and social change continue to present themselves in the forms of schools, public institutions, housing, and public spaces, their political and architectural consequences remain modest and local rather than epic and historic. Today, interest in the spatiostructural and performative potential of synthetic materials, organic technologies, and digital modes of fabrication may manifest itself in works that are weak rather than strong, informal rather than formal, projects that are nonlinear, decentralized, amorphous, and dynamic. These differences are symptomatic of today's network society, in which distributed logics have redefined the modality not only of economic and cultural production but of change, innovation, and social responsibility. Materials and material practices in architecture, as in any other form of culture, can no longer be considered political in themselves but rather assume political charge—often for only a brief moment—through their participation in the systems of communication and consumption that constitute the developed world. To imagine the political potential of architecture in this context, let alone to realize it, remains a task to be undertaken.

From left: Ludwig Mies van der Rohe, convention hall, Chicago, Illinois, 1953–54, collage of interior showing the 1952 Republican Party convention; Konrad Wachsmann, aircraft hangar for the U.S. Air Force, 1959

Toshiko Mori

Materiality and Culture

The history of materials is closely intertwined with the story of human civilization. By tracing the evolution of materials, one can find insights into politics and history. For instance, in Mesopotamia, clay was used to store water and food as well as to record knowledge and events. Today, one of the vital constituents of clay—silicon—is used to embed information in computer chips.[1] As Fernand Braudel writes in *The Structures of Everyday Life*, "At the very deepest levels of material life, there is at work a complex order, to which the assumptions, tendencies and unconscious pressures of economies, societies and civilizations all contribute."[2]

An example of such a complex order can be found in the history of weaving, a technology that dates to the sixth millennium B.C. By tracking the movement of woven materials—silk from China, linen from Egypt, and wool from Mesopotamia—one can learn much about the history of trade. Whereas the Incas in Peru regarded woven patterns as sacred objects, in other cultures weaving was a modest activity typically carried out by women or prisoners of war. Many cultures have also used weaving architecturally to fabricate houses. The Pygmies in central Africa make a recyclable, pliable, permeable, and water-resistant dwelling unit that derives its strength and durability from flexibility rather than rigidity.[3]

Today, weaving continues to be an area of innovation. A technique that translates easily between high- and low-tech, weaving can be done manually, mechanically, or digitally. The first computer punch card was modeled after the cards used to "program" Jacquard looms. The word *digital* stems etymologically from "digits" or fingers. The binary system in an electronic circuit is analogous to the logic of warp and weft in weaving. In A Piece of Cloth (A-POC), a clothing line designed by Issey Miyake, seams and patterns are woven digitally into the fabric. The cloth is then transformed into clothing through the cutting away of fabric rather than the usual stitching together. Woven materials have found numerous industrial applications: steel is spun into yarn for armor and conveyor belts, woven into metal fabrics and chain mesh for filters, and twisted and braided into multilayered cables for use in suspension bridges. Weaving allows otherwise contradictory performance criteria to be achieved in one material. In geotextiles, for instance, as used in landscape design, a top layer prevents soil erosion while tubes underneath facilitate drainage.

The military is one of the main sponsors of materials research. American soldiers in Iraq wear heat-resistant Kevlar uniforms and composite Kevlar-and-carbon helmets that are lighter and stronger than steel. Another military invention is a tightly woven inflatable fabric beam that can be a component of a portable aircraft hangar spanning ninety feet and rising up to thirty-three feet.[4] Air is combined with textiles and becomes a structural element, thus requiring less of the material itself.

Since the 1970s, builders of advanced racing yachts have completely changed their fabrication materials from solid wood to artificial textiles: fiberglass, Kevlar, and carbon fibers. Weaving is crucial to enhancing the performance of these engineered materials. Whereas the individual fibers are anisotropic—that is, dependent on the direction of the fiber for strength—stitching layers of fibers together or laying them in contrasting directions allows boatmakers to attain the desired binary or isotropic behavior. Today, boat builders use the tools and language of tailors, employing fabric and scissors in place of hammers and nails.

Weaving may have contemporary architectural applications as well. In my design for a visitors center to accompany Frank Lloyd Wright's Darwin Martin House (1904),

structure, insulation, electrical conduits, and other infrastructure are woven "organically" into the plate and skin of the inverted hip roof. The roof performs multiple functions: it expresses the public nature of the visitors center, introduces daylight into the interior space, holds snow that can act as insulation when needed, and provides water that can be saved for irrigation. I have reinterpreted Wright's tenet of organic architecture in contemporary terms to mean not a romantic naturalism but the integration of structure, material, and infrastructure through advanced technology and engineering.

Technology and innovative materials abound in our time but unfortunately are only rarely applied to architecture. The reasons for this are largely economic. Unlike more disposable consumer products such as soda bottles and pickle jars, which respond to frequent shifts in demand, buildings are made to last twenty to twenty-five years—roughly the average mortgage cycle—and thus offer a discouragingly slow rate of return to investments in innovation. Funding for research into new materials is directed toward civil engineering—a field that far surpasses architecture in the sheer quantity of materials used—and toward products with military or space applications. Since the criteria for material innovation are increasingly performance-based, new products are stealthy in appearance, designed to be used "invisibly," with no outward indication of their properties. In the future the expression and overt use of new materials will undoubtedly transform and challenge the aesthetics of the built world.

Architects must be more ingenious, inventive, and imaginative in using material technologies. We should adopt a scavenger mentality, familiarizing ourselves with various modes of fabrication, both low- and high-tech. Information should be shared and not hoarded. We should extend our investigations to such phenomena as light, sound, and smell, furthering our explorations of material culture without expending additional resources.

It is easy for those engaged in scientific materials research to become myopic—focused on details about chemical content and physical properties. Conversely, however, the novelty of new materials has always inspired the dream of substances capable of solving all kinds of problems, as evidenced in the ancient practices of alchemy. Without overestimating the omnipotence of new materials, architects should remain committed to utilizing the progressive potentials of material innovation. Architects are inherently charged with the mission of creating works that are life-enhancing, life-affirming, and life-preserving. The use of technology and technique should always be constructive to human civilization.

1. Stephen L. Sass, *The Substance of Civilization* (New York: Arcade Publishing, 1998), 8–9.
2. Fernand Braudel, *The Structures of Everyday Life* (Berkeley: University of California Press, 1992), 333.
3. Guy Philippart De Foy, *Les Pygmées d'Afrique Centrale* (Roquevaire: Editions Parenthèses, 1984), 74.
4. De Foy, *Les Pygmées,* 66–67.

Issey Miyake and Dai Fujiwara, *A-POC 5, One Piece*

A Micropolitics of Material

I want to approach the topic of politics and material by way of an example rather than a manifesto. In my practice, we work on projects that vary in scale from large stadiums to small residences. In some ways, the impact of a small building may be greater than that of a large one. In a large building, there are numerous influences beyond one's control. With a small project, it is possible sometimes to orchestrate a kind of micropolitics.

For example, in the Hedge House (1998–2001), the client asked us to create a 650-square-meter gallery to display his personal art collection. The gallery sits on the grounds of Wijlre Castle near Maastricht, in the Netherlands, alongside a henhouse, greenhouse, and stable. We were asked to establish a route through this varied and often contradictory terrain. Although the client specified that our intervention should use concrete and glass, the materials palette also included orchids, art, chickens, and a collection of garden tools. The challenge was to weave these diverse elements into the architecture of the building.

Hedge House, Wijlre, The Netherlands, 1998–2001

MATERIAL PRAXIS

Jesse Reiser/Nanako Umemoto

Rather than essentializing materials per se, we are interested in the extended and intricate logic of material practices in architecture, in the way that the intelligence embedded in material itself becomes an active part of the way we generate our work. A wide spectrum of possible materialities and material logics exists within any architectural project. At one end are the immediate qualities of weight, durability, and color—the attributes and performances that everyone recognizes in materials; at the other end of this spectrum are the invisible forces that shape architecture, whether social, political, or economic. The poles of architecture as a material practice are defined by both matter and the external directives imposed by and upon architects. In practice, however, negotiating this spectrum is not simple. Our interest is not just in the pragmatic exchanges across this spectrum but in harnessing models of organization based on matter as an abstract machine.

The medium of this machinic concept is the diagram, which provides an abstract model of materiality. The late architectural critic Robin Evans once commented that "architects don't make buildings, they make drawings and models of buildings." While these instruments remove the architect somewhat from physical construction, they nevertheless amplify his or her effectiveness within a wider field of directives conditioned by material logics, legal limits, and social contracts. For example, one can derive a diagram from a dynamic system like the weather: by closely tracking elements such as temperature, pressure, or wind speed, one can generate an abstract diagram of relationships that is scaleless—or more precisely, that

awaits a scale and materiality. This elastic yet precise diagram can then be applied to other material systems, like architecture.

We use diagrams in our work to produce concrete architectural effects and not as representational devices. Representation always ties meaning to an origin. With diagrams the origin is unimportant; the application is what counts. The misunderstanding people make is that we're building the representation. For instance, we used diagrams of weather to design the space frame system for the West Side Convergence project. These architectural designs are not representations of weather. The relationships mapped in the diagrams and into the space frames are neither exclusive nor reducible to weather; they are, in a sense, generic.

Diagrams allow us to connect dynamic models to particular systems of construction. We use diagrams to manage the interaction of a number of organizational models at multiple scales, from the typological to the tectonic. Typically, we begin with architectural models and types bequeathed to us by modernism; they function as standard types for transformation. Novelty arises when these diagrammatic systems of continuous variation interact with modernist models of simple repetition, producing irruptions of local order in a field. The interaction of these systems generates an increase in information, which leads to more differentiation within the field.

For example, the space frame was originally a homogeneous structural system optimized to achieve longer spans with less material. We ask the system to do more than it was originally meant to do; we ask, for instance, that it incorporate program

by changing its configuration, materiality, and ultimately its identity as a space frame. Moreover, by-products, such as variegated densities of open and closed reticulations, and atmospheric effects are achieved from these differentiations. These by-products are not entirely known until they emerge. The issue, then, is to manage these effects rather than try to predict them. In a way, this kind of material management makes design analogous to other material practices, such as cooking, that are complex and multilayered and yet yield results that can be managed with precision. One can precisely track the points where the system fails and where another system must come into play. This is where an aesthetic intuition is essential—an intuition for making choices or selections relating to the type, capabilities, and limits of various systems. When one pushes a system like the space frame to its extreme, it starts to break down or it actually gets simpler, for instance, by becoming a two-way or slab system. Thus it is possible to track how a system is evolving.

The transformation of these once stable and discrete models of architecture offers promise for an expansion of architectural effects. Indeed, the critical dimension of this direction of work lies in its capacity to extend and free up historically determined models, allowing architects to harness the almost limitless productivity of material flows.

West Side Convergence project, New York, New York, 2000; views of space frame system

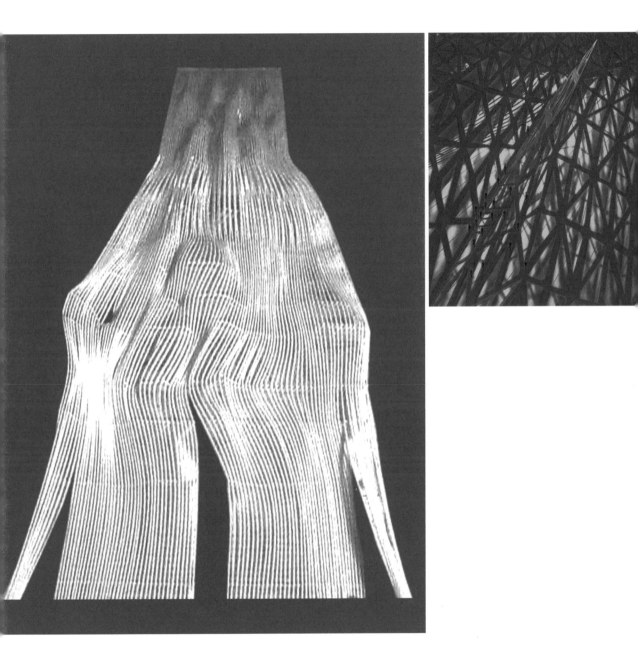

GREEN POLITICS

Victoria Meyers

BUILDING IN REVERSE

Evan Douglis

Throughout history, buildings have featured signs on their facades. The Parthenon's frieze, usually interpreted as depicting the Panathenaic Procession, memorializes the building's function as a center of Athenian life. In Paris, Henri Labrouste inscribed the titles of the books stored in his Bibliothèque Sainte-Geneviève on the building's facade.

Today, governments and corporations are employing a new kind of sign to fashion their images in the public realm: so-called green materials. Examples of such green buildings include Foster and Partners' Swiss Re Headquarters (1997–2004), Foster and Partners' City Hall in London (1998–2002), and Nicholas Grimshaw's British Pavilion for the Seville Expo '92. These architects use new and unusual materials to create envelopes that function in innovative ways, as well as to project a public image.

In the British Pavilion, Grimshaw utilizes water to elegantly transform the facade into a passive solar cooling system. The building wears its theme—climate—on its sleeve. Describing the project, Grimshaw said, "We wanted to express a feeling about the age we live in. We wanted to show our concern about energy, and that we had the ability to reuse all of the materials."[1] The "green" label is as much a sign—in this case, a statement about social conditions—as it is an indication of how the structure operates.

For the Ojai Festival Shell, I designed an organic shape encased within a transparent membrane roof that curves to form part of the facade. The roof is made up of thousands of solar cells that transmit solar energy directly to storage batteries that in turn power the air

conditioning and heating of the stage below. The project is conceived as a large horn. Sound emanates from within the shell to an audience seated on the lawn in front. The boundaries of the project are determined by the distance traveled by sound waves. The architecture relies on natural phenomena both for its form and its functional operation.

In an age marked by the unprecedented destruction of the natural environment, green buildings offer a way for architecture to integrate itself with nature rather than disrupt the ecological field. While the recent popularity of green architecture raises the question of whether such projects are simply window dressings to cover up persistent corporate and governmental misdeeds, the new interest in environmental performance does offer promise. In the city of tomorrow, manmade buildings will be seen as organisms within a larger ecology. This may be the most important way that architecture can influence politics. The future of architecture may lie in nanostructure and skin systems that enable buildings to relate seamlessly to their environments.

1. Nicholas Grimshaw, *Structure, Space and Skin* (London: Phaidon Press, 1993), 62.

We are witnessing a moment in history when vast amounts of energy, political currency, and human life are being sacrificed for the benefit of small populations (on two sides of an ocean) that envision the world as a fundamentalist landscape riddled with absolute truths. How does one understand the radical upheaval that spread across the globe following September 11, 2001, a day on which tools were turned into weapons, architecture into targets, and innocent people into ideological casualties? How is the state of architecture affected by an ethical crisis of such proportions?

Although the attack on the World Trade Center was patently an act of aggression, it is important to note that "unmaking the material world" does not result from political warfare only. Paul Virilio speaks of our society's preoccupation with the "dissolution of matter" as symptomatic of an excess of spectacle: "the hyperacceleration of historical space passing through the delirious machinery of media consumption." Ours is no longer an economy seeking to fulfill the needs of a modernizing society but a culture driven by the perpetual pursuit of need, novelty, and endless difference. As architects committed to sustaining memory through physical forms, how do we define a material practice during an era marked by conflict and dissolution?

Detail + Identity

Why are architects so obsessed with details? The great modernist architect Mies van der Rohe is reputed to have personally sorted through the individual bricks at the construction site of the Lange House, separating the longer blocks from the shorter ones. This sort of fastidiousness, while not atypical among architects, might be considered excessive to those outside the field.

Within architecture, detail has a more specific connotation than simply minute attention to particular items. The architectural detail is typically the place where two materials meet, creating a problem of seams or boundaries. Resolving these points of confrontation occupies untold millions of hours and yields almost as many solutions. Some architects are known to fetishize details, whereas others are considered "sloppy" detailers. The conventions for dealing with details have also changed—from the use of molding to cover seams to the design of reveals that leave a gap between materials, literally "revealing" the joint, and most recently to the creation of curved surfaces that appear seamless.

Architects seem to love details in part because what distinguishes their work from mere building is precisely the careful contemplation and labor that go into a detail. The detail is a site of excess: the point where something is no longer just about utility or function but begins to carry meaning. Thus the attention to details might reflect concerns about identity—not only the identity or meaning of the materials being joined but of architecture itself.

Laurie Hawkinson introduces the subject of detail and identity by clarifying these terms, tracing their origins, and hinting at a possible connection, using the example of a weekend house. A contemporary architect whose work is renowned for its intricate and inventive detailing, Thom Mayne discusses the way that working at an intimate scale has allowed him to infuse more generic designs with moments of singularity.

Michael Bell adopts a different approach to the detail. Drawing on examples from literature, history, and his own work, he meditates on the way that architecture can represent and perhaps alleviate forms of social alienation. Looking back to the debates about architectural style that took place in Germany in the nineteenth century, Andrew Benjamin traces the ways in which style comes to be associated with national identity, pointing to the question: what might a cosmopolitan architecture look like today?

Sylvia Lavin updates the identity of architecture with a meditation on how it became "cool," suggesting that the power of architecture in the twenty-first century may lie in the timeliness of its effects. Finally, Scott Marble and Yolande Daniels both examine the detail and its relationship to modes of production. Marble reflects on the way that new technologies of production enable the design of details to be integrated with manufacturing processes, while Daniels asks how different kinds of detailing, that of contemporary seamless surfaces, for example, might express attitudes toward the labor of production.

Evidence of Identity

I want to begin by defining the terms *detail* and *identity*. What is a detail? In its everyday usage, "paying attention to detail" implies approaching matters item by item, or attending only to the particulars instead of engaging the whole. Within architecture and the arts, a detail is a minute or subordinate part of a building, sculpture, or painting, as distinct from the general concept. The verb "to detail," meaning "to describe through the particulars," comes from the French word *détailler,* which means "to cut into pieces."

What is identity? One definition of identity is the quality or condition of being the same in substance, composition, nature, properties, or particular qualities under consideration. But identity also implies the opposite: individuality, something that distinguishes a person, building, or object. What does identity mean for architecture? The pairing of detail and identity seems to suggest a simultaneous taking apart and putting together—the fragment and the whole considered at once.

Is it possible that an architectural detail can reveal more than just the resolution of materials? Can a fragment of a building provide an entrance into a particular way of thinking? Details can perhaps be seen as a kind of evidence; therefore, buildings and architecture might be thought of as accumulations of material evidence.

In designing a weekend house in Damascus, Pennsylvania, our office, Smith-Miller + Hawkinson Architects, began by asking some basic questions about the building's identity: What is a weekend house? A minimum residence with maximum mobility? Can you represent mobility? What is both a maximum and minimum condition for a house?

The rural house features what the city dwelling doesn't have: views, open space, and a more informal relationship between inside and outside. And yet, the weekend house always latently refers to the city. In our design of the MAXmin House, we wanted to explore how a weekend house, rather than leaving everything behind, could carry with it some of the formality and cultural devices of an urban dwelling: the efficiency and compactness of a city apartment, the open casualness of loft living, the single secured point of entry, and an uneasiness about the ground. In the weekend house, the detail became the site for answering, or at least opening up, such questions about the identity of the house.

MAXmin House, Damascus, Pennsylvania, 1993

Thom Mayne

MOMENTS OF INTENSITY

The notion of working at an intimate scale has been a preoccupation of mine for twenty-five years. Octavio Paz defined craftsmanship not in terms of economy or function but in terms of a pleasure that arose from moving back and forth between utility and beauty. One of the challenges I faced as a young architect practicing in the United States was maintaining control over the production of my creative output. And so, twenty-five years ago, I began producing small-scale objects that were responsive to the human body—a table that moved rhythmically in response to the weight or the activity of its use—or site-specific objects, like a light that was only useful for a particular condition in a building. These objects were sometimes tongue-in-cheek, such as a guard lamp that growled and moved at passersby.

I have also been interested in basic daily rituals. In the Blades House, for example, we created a his-and-hers shower mechanism that related to the day-to-day use of the domestic environment and was juxtaposed with more generic building elements. In projects like this, architecture is understood as a series of intimate engagements, as something experienced haptically, by operating or moving through it, rather than via an intellectual or visual conceptualization. A large amount of our work for a number of years comprised these discrete objects: a door handle that dealt differently with entry and exit, a hand-operated window/door that juxtaposed a large-scale architectural piece with the scale and strength of the human hand.

These armatures became part of a larger generative fabric as we aggressively pursued methods of production that departed from conventional construction techniques. A huge amount of invention took place through the process of construction itself rather than through the traditional conceptual realm.

Much of our work was inspired by machinery and the mechanical processes that interested me as a young man. Details became opportunities to fulfill desires that were isolated from the broader aspirations of the work. These fragments afforded us the opportunity to express an intensity that couldn't be captured in the totality of the work. Within a generic building, one could insert moments of singularity.

All of this has led us to a broader idea of architecture as a collection of fragments, as something open-ended, unfinished, and continually evolving. Our work has become more intricate recently, as the notion of micro or of the specificity of the intimate is increasingly integrated with the work's larger aspirations. At this point, I am trying to blur or find a continuous flow between the generic and the specific, and to integrate localized moments of intensity within a broader design strategy.

From top: Door handle at Kate Mantilini restaurant, Beverly Hills, California, 1986; Tsunami Asian Grill, Las Vegas, Nevada, 1999

Michael Bell

Far Rockaway, New York City

Market Identity: Disappeared by Detail

In *Light in August,* William Faulkner describes the languid, heat-soaked tributaries of dirt roads and mill towns in the American South through a character named Lena. Lena occupies events before and after they occur. "That far within my hearing before my seeing," she states quietly as a wagon that will carry her to the next town breaches a hill.[1] Spatial dimensions are simultaneously affirmed and made relative as Lena separates the inputs from her perceptual senses. In this moment of suspension between past and future circumstance, bodily position is destabilized and financial poverty and social crisis are momentarily alleviated.

In 1937, seven years after the publication of *Light in August,* the United States Housing Act began to transform poverty in northern cities, allocating $800 million in federal loans to states to develop housing for the urban poor.[2] New York City alone received $300 million in federal funds, and the newly formed New York City Housing Authority became an epicenter of urban design and development. Modern architecture and urban design were coupled with federal policies that were portrayed as quasi-socialist and anti-market by banking associations and private developers. In fact, these policies never contravened the market but instead sustained it by housing those whom the market could not or would not support. The racial and economic identities constructed and maintained by these policies and building programs segregated the predominantly African American poor from broader urban society. The housing developments, while formally derived from European models that were socialist in origin, were not anti-market so much as non-market. They were peripheral spaces—adjacent to major capital economies but nevertheless excluded from participating in the means of production and exchange.

In Vienna, the Karl Marx Hof was completed in 1928, two years prior to the publication of Faulkner's novel. The Social Democratic party, already weakened beyond effectiveness, was unable to carry through the building's political ambitions, and the completed edifice eventually became a symbol of absent socialist goals. In Vienna, as in the United States, modern housing was materialized but stripped of its political intentions.

Robert Musil's *The Man without Qualities* was published in Vienna in 1932, virtually concurrent with Faulkner's work. It too unfolds through the spatial and temporal intuitions of a character alienated from his circumstances. For Musil, the site is an emerging twentieth-century European metropolis; for Faulkner, it is the languid American South, with its alternating agrarian and mercantile landscapes. Musil's central character, Ulrich, precipitously falls out of the choreography of metropolitan time. Searching for his own attributes, Ulrich feels as if he is "two separate people." Whereas Lena dwells by "serene rules in a world where reality did not exist,"[3] Ulrich occupies a chasm in an otherwise seamless metropolis.

Musil and Faulkner both evoke subjects who are alienated from the social, political, and economic processes that might sustain identity. Isolated, they seek new sets of social relations and communications. Unlike the buildings of their time, which are helplessly drained of their political origins, Faulkner's and Musil's characters find ways to compensate for distance and to create new forms of identity.

In 2001, the Architectural League of New York invited me to lead a team from Columbia to respond to a request for proposals (RFP) issued by the New York Department of Housing Preservation and Development (NYHPD). The RFP called for the development of mar-

ket-rate two-family housing on a hundred-acre oceanfront site, the Arverne Urban Renewal Area (URA), located on the Far Rockaway Peninsula. Arverne is a barrier island wracked by state-designed poverty housing and outmoded forms of urban renewal. The property is currently owned by the NYHPD and is surrounded by city-, state-, and federally assisted housing. The 308-acre Arverne URA was cleared in the mid-1960s but never redeveloped as conflicts subsumed the site and developers resisted building near existing public housing. In many ways, the area is a hybrid of Faulkner's and Musil's rural and metropolitan settings.

The NYHPD is in the unique position of working toward its own disappearance; it aims to distribute all of its land and assets—held since the near bankruptcy of the city in the mid-1970s—into public/private partnerships. The NYHPD strategy reflects the federal trend toward increasing reliance on public/private partnerships to build low-income housing. Between 1996 and 2000, more than 51,000 public housing rental units in the United States were razed or converted to subsidized private housing. The transformation of public housing to market housing, however, has led to other complexities: in the transition, state forms of identity have been replaced with market forms of identity—or lack thereof—and architecturally speaking, lack of detail.

The new housing at Arverne strives to be stateless: while state funds will contribute to the development, they will be folded into a private market framework. Unlike the residential fabric that surrounds the site, this new housing will not reveal or sustain its subsidies. Rockaway, an unfortunate refuge for a concentrated population of African Americans living below the poverty line, will be deconcentrated by the new quasi-traditional housing. As in

Faulkner's and Musil's novels, in the absence of traditional social and political relationships, alienation may give rise to new combinations and forms of time and space. Can architecture alone help to alleviate the kinds of estrangement depicted by Musil and Faulkner? Can buildings compress distance and contribute to the construction of new identities? Or does placing this burden on architecture set it up for the same apparent failure that was presumed to have been endemic to the existing modern housing?

Rafael Moneo provides a touchstone for our project at Arverne: in describing the separation of working and dwelling spaces in the modern city, Moneo argues that the problem of the city becomes that of the house. The house is a representation of the city, and dwelling is an urban condition. Moneo borrows from Aldo Rossi in claiming that architecture can compensate for distance and time, thereby helping to overcome circumstance. Architecture offers a "glimpse" of the city beyond local boundaries. At Arverne, we have tried to produce housing that suggests space beyond the isolation of local site borders, beyond the borders of inadequate income and low education levels. In their details, these buildings attempt to undermine the political and economic systems that have isolated Arverne from greater New York and to address not only the economic impoverishment and rural alienation embodied in Faulkner's vast landscapes but also the urban and philosophical poverty of Musil's metropolitan experience. Architects have yet to grapple with both of these forms of destitution, and to produce a truly modern form of housing for America's poorest populations.

1. William Faulkner, *Light in August* (1932; New York: Vintage International, 1990), 473.
2. Robert A. Caro, *The Power Broker* (New York: Vantage Books, 1974), 611.
3. Faulkner, *Light in August,* 473.

Andrew Benjamin

THE STYLE OF ARCHITECTURE

In order for part of the past to be touched by the present instant there must be no continuity between them.
  Walter Benjamin, *The Arcades Project*

Writing within the context of the German style debates of the nineteenth century, Heinrich Hübsch issued a pamphlet in 1828 entitled *Im welchem Style sollen wir bauen?* ("In what style should we build?").[1] In contrast to Johann Winckelmann, who argues that "There is but one way for the moderns to become great and perhaps unequalled . . . by imitating the ancients (*die Nachahmung der Alten*),"[2] Hübsch's pamphlet begins with the following formulation: "Painting and sculpture have long since abandoned the lifeless imitation of antiquity. Architecture has yet to come of age and continues to imitate the antique style (*den antiken Styl nachzuahmen*)."[3] What is significant about this formulation is the positioning of architecture as outside the modern—it "has yet to come of age"—and the defining of that position in relation to style. Once identified in these terms, the range of possible responses is set up in advance.

This attempt to break the determining hold of imitation is a recurrent motif. It occurs in its most emphatic form in those conceptions of the modern that ground its inception in an inaugurating interruption. Hübsch's pamphlet finishes with a restatement of the contemporary dilemma and obligation of architecture: "In every case buildings logically designed in their basic elements will rank much higher as works of art (*als Kunstwerke*), even with the most infelicitous decorations, than the most exact imitations (*die getreuften Nachahmungen*) of ancient art."[4]

At the center of Hübsch's argument is the twofold move in which the activity of the imagination comes to be championed at the same time that a simple miming of ancient styles is put aside. Style comes to the fore as a question, and with it comes the necessity to control the excesses of the imagination and to avoid the idiosyncratic, an eventuality that cannot be precluded once the sense of continuity guaranteed by imitation is broken. Karl Bötticher's contribution to the debate, in a pamphlet written in 1846, reinforces the impossibility of defining

"style" in terms of individual aspirations. However, neither that move nor the redefinition of style in terms of tectonic possibilities can be taken as ends in themselves. The question of style is tied up with another element: the national question. This is the definitive way of avoiding particularity and accounts for why Bötticher argues in regard to style that "Only a whole nation can cause its inception." Moreover, a style may take an "epoch for its development."[5] Not only is style tied to the question of the nation, it is equally part of the nation's history.

What emerges is a complex state of affairs in which the break with imitation allows for the national question to be part of modernity. In other words, the impossibility of maintaining continuity through time, and the necessity of a break within natural time—a break that constitutes the modern—once articulated within a concern with style, become insistent forms of the national question. While Bötticher, at a given moment, connects style with nationhood, the break with imitation allows style to have a projective quality. The use of style and ornamentation may project—in the sense of "aim to construct"—a nation's self-conception (not the nation at hand, but the nation to come). This should not be seen as an aberrant possibility but as another way through the predicament of modernity, at the point that the latter is understood as a break. Once a return cannot be made and continuity is no longer an option, then the question of how to continue cannot be avoided. This is the locus within which the question of style emerges.

The complex relationship between style and national identity continues to define how style is understood throughout the early part of the twentieth century. For example, in a lecture called "Kunst und Technik" given by the German modernist architect Peter Behrens in 1910, the two terms are still defined in relation to one another: "By style we mean only the unified formal expression (*den einheitlichen Formausdruck*), the manifestation of the entire spiritual life of an epoch (*den die gesamten Geistäusserungen einer Epoche ergaben*). Unified character, not the particular or the peculiar, is the decisive factor."[6]

There are two points that need to be made here. The first is that the interarticulation of style and the national question is a consequence of the interruption that signals the presence of the modern and is announced in architectural terms by the severance of the immediate connection between style and appearance. The second is that due to this severance, the link between style and the national question does not exhaust the question of style because the link is merely a contingent relation. The presence of this contingency means that the appearance of modern architecture remains a question whose answer is always to be determined. Moreover, the subsequent recasting of the modern as International Style becomes another contingent connection: the International Style simply replaces the national. Therefore, a critique of the identification of the modern with the International Style cannot occur by a return to the national.

What emerges, in brief, is an opening. Between the national and the international—both of which can be understood as responses to the question of style—there arises another formulation of both style and place. Developing it means giving serious attention to the question of what a cosmopolitan architectural style would be.[7]

Posed in these terms, the question of modern architecture, once articulated within the cosmopolitan, moves architecture beyond the image while still allowing for the image of architecture. A complex interplay of design procedures, materials, and a reconfiguration of site must be central within any determination of how the cosmopolitan would appear. And yet, it will never be just an appearance—mere image. Since the movements between design and its realization, the relations between geometry and materials, and finally the transformation of the site such that geography becomes architectural all raise the question of appearance, it is also the case that appearance—architecture's material presence—will have a modality that cannot have been determined in advance. This is the legacy bequeathed to design by the interruptive force of Hübsch's question.

This discussion is extracted from a work in progress, *Style and Time: Essays on the Politics of Appearance.* Central to this project is the argument that the style debate in Germany provides a locus in which to discuss the emergence of modern architecture. That emergence is bound up with the necessary severance of style from appearance. This severance is the implicit generator of the debate. The majority of the texts comprising the debate can be found in English in *In What Style Should We Build? The German Debate on Architectural Style,* ed. Wolfgang Herrmann (Santa Monica, Calif.: Getty Center, 1992).

1. Heinrich Hübsch, *Im Welchem Style Sollen Wir Bauen?* (Karlsruhe, 1828; English trans., Herrmann, *In What Style Should We Build?*). Page references to Hübsch are given first to the German edition and then to the English.
2. Hübsch, 2, 60.
3. Hübsch, 65, 1.
4. Hübsch, 100, 52.
5. Herrmann, *In What Style Should We Build?*, 157.
6. The text of this lecture appears in Tilman Buddensieg, *Industriekultur Peter Behrens und die AEG 1907–1914* (Berlin: Mann Verlag, 1979), 278–85. The particular passage quoted is on page 279.
7. For a discussion of the nature of the cosmopolitan and its possible position within architecture, see my "The 'Place' of Cosmopolitan Architecture," *Architectural Theory Review* 7, no. 1 (2002).

Sylvia Lavin

How Architecture Stopped Being the 97-Pound Weakling and Became Cool

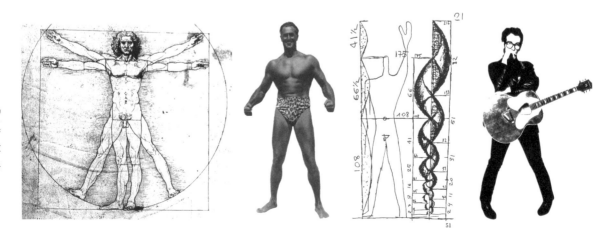

While the growing popularity of architecture over the past decade is often commented upon—evidence cited normally ranges from Bilbao to HGTV (Home and Garden Television)—no one has particularly argued that a correlate to this increase is that architecture is now cool. Prima facie evidence for architecture's recent coolness might include the Prada store, *Wallpaper* magazine, and Columbia's School of Architecture. I don't mean cool in Marshall McLuhan's sense of media with low content and high participation or in the sense of aesthetic heat loss. I mean cool in its everyday sense of an elusive yet durable, generic yet personal desire. The word itself, which encapsulates a rich set of cultural nuances, admixtures, and origins, above all embodies a complex relation to time and timeliness. Cool epitomizes the transience of slang, but it is also one of slang's longest-lived terms. While not everyone admits to wanting to be cool, and while many would profess disdain at a desire so superficial and fleeting, most people would not wish to be permanently uncool. Architecture has a theoretical arsenal of historic proportions with which to resist the pull of the cool, but despite its best efforts, the most interesting aspects of contemporary architecture are those that have succumbed and have become cool.

Coolness is the product of a slippery relation between an object, its use, its mode of production, and its mode of reception. A cool person can make an uncool object cool, but an uncool person may or may not be cooled up by a cool object. Despite its unreliability, the effects of cool can be formidable. Putting the right pair of glasses on the ninety-seven-pound weakling—the archetype of the uncool body—can reorganize him or her into the epitome of cool. Cool is a confluence of forces that works through the apparently unpredictable elisions between the state of the subject, the agency of the object, and

the effects of design. Cool is provisional, temporary, and undermined as an aesthetic category by the always different individual sense of what is cool. That's what makes cool post-critical rather than neo-modern.

When modernism wanted to banish the ninety-seven-pound weakling it did so by making him beautiful: by invoking an absolute, an aesthetic ideal, the myth of progress, mastery of the body, and American can-do. Charles Atlas literally incorporated modernism into a perfected body. The appeal of Elvis Costello, on the other hand, lies not in some authenticating body but in his provisional cool, which resides in his surfaces, in the curating of his "look." Cool is a matter of design rather than of birth or hard work. It is an effect, and effects are conditions that are detachable from the logic of causality. The greater the distance between the cause and effect, or the less their link is perceptible, the greater the sense of effectiveness. That's why Elvis Costello needs his glasses: they are not the cause of his cool, but they are his cool special effect.

Because cool is an effect rather than an ideal or a rationale or a meaning, it's unreliable. The glasses trick doesn't always work, but that doesn't mean its effects are ineffective. Cool is better understood as a vector than as a static condition. The Costello glasses move toward the cool rather than stand still as a legible index of the cool. This is like the difference between modernist transparency and contemporary luminescence. Modernist transparency appeared as directly and causally linked to the material properties of glass: the modern movement made glass into a magic writing tablet and rationalized the material's effects. Contemporary luminescence, on the other hand, is an effect whose cause is not immediately visible, and is one that would be dissipated by enhanced legibility. Effects are dissembling,

provisional, and contemporary. Special effects are especially conditional and experimental—like 1950s Formica or a Replicant in *Blade Runner,* they sense their impending demise. But in incorporating an expiration date, their shelf life, however short, can be especially vivid. Special effects thus claim for themselves the moment of now.

Reyner Banham argued that the task of the historian was to project the immediate future. My task in this context is to identify those intense forms of contemporaneity that are consequently cool. I'm on what Malcolm Gladwell would call "a cool hunt," and while I may not be able to define perpetual cool, I can say something about the nature of the hunt. Since cool is an effect, not a thing, the hunter must be mindful of sensibilities, and in particular of how (or whether or not) cool affects contemporaneity. Contemporaneity is not a default; because someone exists now does not mean that that person is contemporary, just as cool glasses cannot guarantee that they will produce a cool person. Cool is not the same as zeitgeist, a mysterious yet reliable force that was thought to permeate everything with the aura of modernity. Although some things were thought to have more zeitgeist than others, it was nevertheless considered to be a unifying principle. All things had zeitgeist at least to some degree, and it was the historian's job to reveal it when it was hidden. Not everything is cool; in fact, some things are definitively uncool. And cool never needs revealing since it always lies on the surface: even failed attempts to be cool are perfectly manifest. Most important, cool is never retrograde or simply neo-modern. Cool is always contemporary.

From left: The classical body as drawn by Leonardo da Vinci; Charles Atlas®, "The World's Most Perfectly Developed Man"®; Le Corbusier's Modulor; Elvis Costello

DETAIL AND PRODUCTION
Scott Marble

DETAIL AND ARTICULATION
Yolande Daniels

Techniques of dimensional and geometric representation such as drawing and model building typically constitute processes distinct and independent from construction. However, technology now allows design information to be embedded in production and assembly processes, leading to an integrated system. Although still mediated through forms of abstract representation, CNC (computer numerically controlled) systems bring the process of design closer to the production of buildings, merging them through a common language of information. The architectural detail is largely a product of the relationship of design to industry. If the modernist detail was based on negotiating tolerances between premanufactured building components that were then assembled, today we are shifting to methods of production that are based on the management and organization of information, where tolerances are numerically controlled and fully integrated during production.

One of the ongoing debates surrounding factory-built housing in the second half of the last century was whether to produce the entire house or only certain parts. After years of working toward his goal of an affordable factory-built house, Walter Gropius came to this assessment in 1964: "Genuine variety without monotony could have been attained if we had taken greater interest and influence in the development and design of an ever more comprehensive production of standardized, component building parts which could have been assembled into a wide diversity of house types. Instead the idea of prefabrication was seized by manufacturing firms who came up with the stifling project of mass producing whole house types instead of component parts only." [1]

In Gropius's view, by the end of the twentieth century manufacturing and industry had taken over the promise of the marriage of production and architecture, resulting in homogeneity. Today, recent innovations in production technologies that enable considerations of detail and assembly to be embedded into production processes may offer architects a way to achieve, in Gropius's words, "genuine variety without monotony."

1. Walter Gropius, quoted in Herbert Gilbert, *The Dream of the Factory-Made House: Walter Gropius and Konrad Wachsmann* (Cambridge, Mass.: MIT Press, 1984), 318.

It has been suggested that the genealogy of the architectural detail extends from the premodern molding to the modern reveal to the postmodern expressed detail and to postpostmodern seamlessness. The molding veils differences and the labor of production by compensating for or expressing them, while the reveal disguises by negating or suppressing them. The expressed detail exposes the act of articulation itself, or perhaps an overcompensation or overproduction, while the isomorphic polysurface (blob) suppresses the detailing of the surface in internalized infrastructure and produces an abstraction or seamlessness that is apparently dissociated from its means of production.

Although the seamless model appears to be without detail, is it possible to consider a detail that is not subservient to function but rather expresses the intelligence of the lines that map or regulate the surface? And if we accept that topological (blob) tectonics internalize their details, how might we interpret the need for (dis)sections to reveal the details of the processes, labor, and techniques used to produce the seemingly seamless surface and to articulate the intelligence or protocols of the system?

The twentieth century was a period of unprecedented formal inventiveness in architecture—from the abstract compositions imagined by the Russian Constructivists to the billowing metallic shapes of Frank Gehry's Guggenheim Museum in Bilbao, Spain. With the generation of each new form, however, the question persists: does formal innovation affect the larger social world? Even today, the phrase "form for form's sake" lingers as a kind of indictment against design solipsism.

Form implies a set of issues and explorations internal to architecture. Strange new shapes may inspire delight but, conversely, may appear excessive, impractical, or even frivolous. How, then, does form relate to broader audiences, issues, and agendas? Should architects even try to claim political, economic, or social effects for their creations? What is the value of avant-garde form?

Examining recent calls in architectural design for greater formal autonomy, Mary McLeod suggests that it is only through the interplay of form and function that architecture gains a larger influence. Frank Gehry, one of the most celebrated formal innovators of the twentieth century, discusses the way that power—real or imagined—may be detrimental to the creative process. Architects, he says, should stop worrying so much about the consequences of their actions and simply allow themselves the freedom to invent.

The work of Odile Decq can also certainly be described as formally innovative, and yet the architect herself explicitly disavows form as a principal concern. For her, form is a by-product of other pursuits, such as pleasure, and is always shaped by the particularities of context.

In contrast to Decq, Alejandro Zaera-Polo argues that architecture cannot be understood as a consequence of external processes but should retain a degree of autonomy. He uses the concepts of typology and species to rejuvenate a search for architectural possibilities from within the terms of the discipline. Like Zaera-Polo, Jeffrey Kipnis is interested in the notion of species, but rather than promoting a specific approach to form-making, he challenges architects more broadly to begin investigating a notion of sameness.

Reflecting on the events of September 11, 2001, Peter Eisenman considers what possibilities remain for architecture once the current languages of expression are exhausted and argues for the exploration of new languages of creation. Like Eisenman, Karl Chu emphasizes the creative or generative aspect of architecture. Chu advocates a "morphogenetic" approach to design, drawing on the algorithmic logic of genetics to develop new forms for the twenty-first century.

Mary McLeod

Form and Function Today

The first definition given in the dictionary of the word *form* is simply "shape" or "configuration." In architecture, then, *form* refers to the shape or morphology of a building; it is the configuration of its physical matter, apart from its actual material properties. But it also means more than that in architecture, alluding to that which is beyond function. A building's formal attributes are its aesthetic properties. One meaning of form, now archaic, is beauty, which was traditionally associated with style and decoration. Since the beginning of the modern movement and Adolf Loos's condemnation of ornament, form has referred instead to compositional relations, such as solid and void, rhythm, proportion, repetition, counterpoint, balance—the abstract properties of design that give a work its spatial and visual quality. In fact, it might even be said that form is what separates building from architecture; it results from those self-conscious compositional techniques that endow materials, structure, and program with artistic qualities. It is the art in architecture. In this respect, form is a kind of excess, an unfunctional addition, "purposeful purposelessness" in Kantian terms. Of course, the most *sachlich* strain of the modern movement rejected this excess. For hard-core functionalists, such as Hannes Meyer and the G group, architecture was building.

However, even the most mundane, utilitarian buildings have form, since matter without form does not exist. Form is intrinsic to both building and architecture. Moreover, what is immediately obvious in architecture, but is not always apparent in the seemingly freer, more autonomous arts such as music, painting, and sculpture, is that form and function—function now taken broadly to include any social, political, or cultural purpose—are never completely distinct. Even in the most hermetic works of art, form gains a purpose; as Theodor Adorno so succinctly put it in his Werkbund lecture of 1965, "The illusion of purposelessness has its own purpose."[1]

This has become all the more apparent in our ever-expanding commodity culture; few can sustain the belief that art is a utopian enclave apart from social reality or that there is such a thing as disinterested form. With postmodernism and its pluralistic artistic practices, form has lost its imperative as a privileged historical strategy or even as necessarily the most important part of art. It is not surprising that architecture was among the first of the disciplines to make this condition evident. But just as form can never be completely separated from function, it is equally clear that function requires some kind of form—not simply in an "organicist" sense, as something developing quasi-spontaneously from within ("form follows function") but as something consciously imposed by the architect's or builder's will, even if that intention has only a mediated relation to form's social role. To return to the distinction between building and architecture, one might even say that part of the architect's task is to give form to function, to make it more than function. Architecture accommodates function, but it also interprets and potentially expands and transforms function. That is a fundamental dimension of its influence.

Neo-avant-garde tendencies (at least at some architecture schools, such as Columbia and UCLA) have tended to split form and function. On the one hand, we have seen a return to a kind of biotechnical determinism, a vision of organic mechanism that regards the computer as a means of realizing the effervescent dream of total functionalism. On the other hand, we also have—despite postmodern notions of pluralism, intertextuality, and contamination—a persistent formalism, where form is seen as autonomous, whether generated by intuitive criteria, typology, or syntactic research.

Both approaches risk a certain hermeticism and solipsism. The biotechnical tendency, represented at its most extreme by Karl Chu's morphogenetic model but also more generally by the persistent call for a computer-generated, objective design process, recalls the limitations of the functionalism advocated by the modern movement and of the design methodologies influenced by 1960s systems theory, notably Christopher Alexander's pattern language. No matter how sophisticated the computer program or how comprehensive the variables to be accommodated, the resultant forms remain removed from actual needs and desires, whether material or symbolic. This is not only because these projects have not been built. What has not been acknowledged fully are the limitations of the computer software, the arbitrariness of the criteria established, the subjectivity of the process of editing form, and the banal sameness of function itself

when narrowly viewed as an a priori tool or codifiable device. Design seems caught between an instrumental determinism and intuitive mysticism. That which is purportedly most objective becomes most subjective and detached from collective social life.

Paradoxically, in this regard the new biotechnical determinism recalls intuitive neoexpressionist approaches, which overtly acknowledge their formal origins. There are also stylistic similarities between the two. Just as the idiosyncratic serial variations of biotechnical approaches have at times produced a relentless sameness—a homogeneity stemming from overwrought particularity without hierarchy—willfully intuitive designs also often result in a certain sameness of style, reminding us how small the innovative dimension of form can ever be. Here, the more restrained models of autonomous form calling for a return to type and "sameness" might seem a welcome alternative, if only for their realism about the limits of formal variation and invention. However, in contrast to typological investigations in the 1960s and 1970s, which were linked to a desire for communication and public legibility, these more recent theoretical models conceive variation (for example, the notion of species) as occurring almost semiautomatically, without conscious intent. Again the rhetoric draws on biological metaphors— breeding, proliferation, mutation, evolution—recalling the determinist strains of the first model. Both tendencies suggest another dimension of form: the formulaic. Fortunately, some of these practitioners are not as willing to dis-

pense with choice, agency, and value in their architecture as their theoretical position might suggest. In fact, their best built work suggests that a critical conception of function—one that sees function not as fixed and prescribed but as expansive and transformative—can infuse form with a certain life, whether the starting point is an intuitive, highly subjective approach or one based on the syntactic manipulation of autonomous formal types.[2]

Function brings variation and imagination to arbitrary and overly generalized abstract form, just as form brings invention and play to the mechanistic dimensions of an instrumental, codified functionalism. Each potentially challenges the stasis and hermeticism of the other. It is in this dialectical tension between form and function— their ambiguous, complex, and fluid relationship—that much of architecture's potential richness, both aesthetic and social, resides.

1. Theodor W. Adorno, "Functionalism Today," trans. Jane O. Newman and John H. Smith, *Oppositions* 17 (Summer 1979): 33.
2. Adolf Behne made a similar observation about the relationship between function and form in his prescient study of 1923, *The Modern Functional Building*. His comments about organic functionalism also have uncanny relevance to contemporary biotechnical tendencies. Adolf Behne, *Der moderne Zweckbau* (Munich: Drei Masken Verlag, 1926; English ed., *The Modern Functional Building,* trans. Michael Robinson, Santa Monica, Calif.: Getty Research Institute, 1996).

Architecture and Intuition

I was trained as a modernist. I came to school after the Beaux-Arts movement, and all my teachers said, enough with that historic shit. Let's get on with it. I thought that historicism was a dead end. The painters and sculptors were doing stuff that was much more exciting; they were playing with ideas, forms, textures, and feelings that were infinitely more interesting to me. I wanted to discover how to make a building that had what I call juice—that is, feeling or a spirit. If you look at history, you find that over the centuries, numerous artists, sculptors, and architects have struggled to represent movement with inert materials. That was interesting to me. When I looked at sculpture, especially statues of the Indian goddess Shiva, I sensed the movement inside them. Then I thought to myself, cars have movement, planes have movement: there's movement all around us. How do you bring that into architecture? I started messing with those ideas.

Years ago, I did a trellis for Norton Simon. I wanted it to look like frozen motion, but I didn't know how to do it. I could draw and model it, but I didn't know how to build it, exactly, so I convinced Norton to let me construct it in sections. I built the first layer, and that was fine. I built the second layer and half of the third, and I was starting to get somewhere. Then he stopped me. He said he didn't want to spend any more money on my fancy ideas, and that it was going to be my unfinished symphony.

When some people started doing temples again—postmodern stuff—I reacted against it because of the way I was trained. If you're going to go back in history, you might as well go back millions of years—to fish—and I started drawing fishlike things. It was intuitive. I started drawing, and I let it go to see where it would lead. I started making things. I made a thirty-five-foot-long fish sculpture for an exhibition, and I realized that when I stood next to it, I felt the movement. Other people sensed it, too. Even though it was an ugly piece of kitsch, it worked somehow. At thirty-five feet long, it was starting to approach an architectural scale. From there, I cut off the head and tail, and I made a fish room for the Walker Center in Minneapolis, at the request of Mildred Friedman, then curator of design. And it worked. We stripped it of some of the kitsch; we were making it more abstract and it started to work. After I learned how to build that, I took the next step and moved to a larger scale. It wasn't something I sat down and planned. If I knew what I was going to do, I wouldn't bother to do it—it would have been done already in my head.

When I was a kid, I studied the Talmud with my grandfather. The essence of the Talmud is the golden rule: "Do unto others as you would have others do unto you." That's the logic. It's not much more complicated than that. There was another saying when I was growing up: "If you step on a crack, you break your mother's back." So, when you're a kid, you don't step on a crack, because you don't want to break your mother's back. It's a childlike notion of power. I think we carry something of that sensibility into our adult lives; you think that if you stand on a certain place near a fulcrum you can move the universe. But if you go at things that way, your actions become so important and powerful that you can't do anything. You go into gridlock. For instance, I hired a kid who had studied with Peter Eisenman. He was talented, but his experience with Peter had caused him to view each line as so precious that he couldn't draw a line or make a wall. He strove for a perfection that he could never reach, and it paralyzed him. It's wonderful to search your psyche and to comb your life for meaning—for the meaning of the universe. But you're asking more than is humanly possible of yourself. You are a product of nature. If you just follow your intuitions, you won't get out of line because gravity will hold you down. The culture around you, the building department, the economy, and the client will keep you in line, so in all likelihood, you will never destroy the world. You won't break your mother's back if you step on a crack. You can, however, do things that have an effect on the world. You just have to free yourself to let those things happen.

Fisher Performing Arts Center, Bard College, Annandale-on-Hudson, New York, 2003

ARCHITECTURE AND PLEASURE

For me, architecture is always contextual and contingent. Form never comes first. I am not interested in making forms, even if a project inevitably has a form. At the same time, form in architecture is not only the result of external influences. It's a more complex relationship.

Does the environmental debate present a truly new question or only another function to be resolved? Will it lead us to a redefinition of our way of living, and hence to a fundamental reconceptualization of architecture? Does the instability of the world affect architecture directly—influencing forms, height, and urban development—or only indirectly, through new social and political relationships that can change the way we think about architectural spaces? How will these questions affect the fabrication of architectural forms?

At the beginning of the 1990s, transparent facades became popular in France, and architects started to treat glass facades as surfaces instead of as windows in a wall. One architectural critic explained that the Hotel industriel Berlier built by Dominique Perrault along the Paris periphery was transparent because it was an expression of democracy. If we could look through all the buildings from their exteriors and nothing could be hidden inside, the thinking went, this would be democracy. In my view, this is not so much democratic as it is the latest development in the world of social control foreseen by George Orwell. If all buildings were totally transparent, there couldn't be any privacy.

Today architects face a challenge that is more complex than ever: the question of desire and pleasure. Paul Virilio observes that after having addressed function through the creation of new spatial organizations at the beginning of the twentieth century and social needs through the exploration of new uses in the second part of the century, architects are now turning to the notion of pleasure.

What are the new desires of our society? This is perhaps the fundamental political question facing us as

architects. The question of desire and pleasure is complex and never neutral. We are humans and therefore our desires are always evolving. They cannot be controlled and predefined. They are personal and only sometimes collective. They are absolutely contingent and dependent on external influences—global, political, economic, and climatic—as well as on internal conditions such as one's last lunch, health, or love.

Does architecture merely reveal existing contexts, contingencies, and conditions, or can it anticipate and shape new directions through so-called avant-garde forms? I don't like to speak about avant-garde forms because what we usually call avant-garde forms are often only new for an instant and then quickly become "arrière-garde forms." Avant-garde refers too much to a question of fashion. Even though architecture is now more and more instantaneous and temporary rather than built to last forever, its duration is longer than the time of fashion.

In my work, architecture and form are related to the question of pleasure. At the same time, they deal with contexts and the surrounding conditions: politics, economics, culture, and the urban or natural landscape. I don't rely on typologies that embody an abstract point of view and that presuppose that there are universal responses to the questions I am asking. There is no such thing as a general or universal response to a program or a site. Everything is specific.

Furniture for the UNESCO Headquarters conference hall, Paris, France, 2002

Breeding Architecture

Alejandro Zaera-Polo

I want to claim for architecture a certain indispensable interiority. While architectural form undoubtedly influences and is influenced by politics, social dynamics, and culture, it cannot be legitimized or assessed solely on the basis of its external effects. Architecture brings together the material aspects of these spheres through form; form is the plane that provides a level of consistency. For me, the real essence of the practice of architecture is the process of organizing materials in such a way that the form and program of a building become consistent.

Typology offers us a way to assess the practice of architecture as material organization. Architectural types are assemblages of form and program, and typology, the study of the classification of these assemblages, is the framework that traditionally has linked forms of architecture. The problem with typology, of course, is that it has been used in the past as a recipe to reproduce existing conditions, thus making it inadequate for dealing with the increasingly accelerated pace of social, cultural, and political change brought on in part by the processes of globalization. However, typology need not lead to the systematic repetition of existing types. Rather, it can be used to assess whether the work one is doing is moving forward or standing still. Typology can become a catalyst for architectural experimentation and the development of new urban models, especially if we conceive of types as objects for manipulation and adjustment rather than for imitation.

Farshid Moussavi and I have had an ambiguous relationship with typology. Our early practice was based on the assumption that we should avoid resorting to typology as a device or tool to produce architecture. It was Jeff Kipnis who first told us, "Your practice is fundamentally about typology." This led us to rethink our own work.

In our architectural practice as well as in studios we taught at Columbia University and elsewhere, we explored the possibility of reinterpreting typology as a tool for overcoming the limits of authorship or personal style. Over time, another category emerged—the concept of the species. Instead of being associated with the notion of systematic or equal repetition, the species was linked with the processes of mutation and adaptation to different environments—in other words, with changes in time and in space. We felt that this idea of the species could potentially help us overcome the limited definition of typology as something that only produced repetition.

In designing the Yokohama Port Terminal, we created a diagram that began as an attack on typology—specifically, the typology of the terminal—proposing instead that the terminal was a space with its own internal forms of organization. Yet in the process of building the project, typology emerged as a useful way of thinking about the methods of assembly. We based the material organization of the building on the concept of repetition: a small number of details or types were repeated throughout but were differentiated to solve particular situations. We designed the geometry of the building to achieve this, organizing the structural elements into a few types that could be combined to produce a complex form. The typology of the deck generated many different types of decks; the approach to the glazing and fencing was similar. A single detail varies to accommodate particular conditions. The hope was that through the systematic repetition and differentiation of these elements, something previously unknown would emerge.

Recently, we have tried to rethink our practice through the lens of species. We created a phylogenetic diagram in which we separated our past projects into three categories. We were trying to understand the projects as if they were breeds, things that were not designed but that came out of a common order with differentiated individuals. As with horses or wines, successful traits can be selected and the results of cross-breeding can be registered. A coherent practice might emerge from a phylogenetic process in which a few seeds proliferate across different environments over time, generating distinct yet consistent results. We are trying to define our practice neither as a series of experiments that are contingent on particular conditions nor as an imposition of a specific style but rather as a consistent reservoir of architectural species that will proliferate, mutate, and evolve in the years to come. We want to find a way of operating that will be both internally consistent and responsive to external processes. In doing so, we hope to identify new directions for experimentation.

From top: Yokohama Port Terminal, Yokohama, Japan, 2002; phylogenetic diagram of FOA's projects

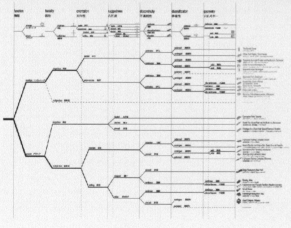

Jeffrey Kipnis

FORM'S SECOND COMING

"You've got it all wrong. You don't need to follow me, you don't need to follow anyone."

"You are all individuals."

"Yes! We are all individuals!"

"You are all different."

"Yes! We are all different!"

"I'm not."

In *Foucault*, Gilles Deleuze writes, "Every form is a compound of relationships between forces. Given those forces, our first question is with what forces from the outside they enter into a relationship, and then what form is created as a result." In *Le Pli*, he writes, "'Good' macroscopic form always depends on microscopic processes." Taken together, I believe these postulates constitute an adequate set of axioms not only for the architectural question of form and influence but also for the more problematic contemporary question of form as such. They condense a physics, history, politics, and ethics into a single calculus and therefore provide a starting point from which to pursue the two requirements of any attempt to formulate the terms of a positive project: process and judgment.

One way to work out the particulars of this calculus for architecture is to reflect on the writings and projects of my colleagues. But there is another course of action—to attempt a speculative leap into the discourse of a near future, one precarious enough to be genuinely risky but not so foolhardy as to be doomed from the outset. The only way I can think to do this is to try to give voice prematurely to one of those unformed pricklings that plagues my thought like a swarm of gnats. To do so, I turn to another of my favorite philosophers, Monty Python, and a scene from his film *The Life of Brian*.

There are two important thinkers in the scene, the ever-popular theorist of individuality ("You are all different") and the contrarian gadfly ("I'm not"). For compelling historical reasons, we have become experts on the discourse of difference. Yet were I to advise the next generation, my gut feeling would be to direct them toward the contrarian, in other words, toward a speculative theory of the same that is as radical in its implications as our theories of difference are today. Though I cannot yet imagine the tenets of such a theory, I will hazard an anecdote or two about it.[1]

Our tacit approach in architecture today is to treat the same as equivalent to identity, that is, as a defective form of difference, or difference equals zero. Such a categorical (essentialist or typological) notion of the same at best tolerates small differences and is therefore inherently conservative, as followers of Leon Krier's argument will appreciate. Yet in other fields, in mathematics and biology, for example, something else is afoot. As we track the evolution of geometry from descriptive to analytic and projective to topology, we see another notion of the same developing. Descriptive geometry, like Krier, sought to establish categories and to construct membership and equivalence tests in order to control difference. With triangles, descriptive geometry gave us definitions—scalene, right, isosceles, and equilateral—and tests for congruence and similarity. Projective geometry abandoned that apparatus in exchange for the power to transform any triangle into another, giving rise to a dynamic rather than categorical theory of the same. Topology took that evolution one step further, abandoning even the originating primitive or elemental shape (the "triangle") in favor of a general manifold—a geometric figure or solid that is not changed by homeomorphisms, such as stretching or bending, as illustrated by the proverbial equivalence of the doughnut and the coffee cup. Topology thus theorizes mathematical sameness in yet more powerful

dynamic terms. Deleuze's choice of the term *multiplicité* is a nod to that project; it is from the French mathematical term for what in English topology is called a manifold. Look at the faces and figures around you: all variations, no original theme. There is the idea of the face to be sure, but no ideal face.

Despite widespread misunderstanding, the efforts by Greg Lynn, Karl Chu, Foreign Office Architects, Asymptote, UN Studio, and others to generate architectural morphological families (or species) with no premised primitive draw deeper impetus from the dynamic premises of mathematical topology than from the aesthetics of shapes. These architects set their research project in contrast to semiotic-process architects like Peter Eisenman, who in directing their work toward reading, must posit an initial primitive, though that primitive need no longer hold the status of a metaphysical or typological origin and may stand for any provisional premise. That primitive is then transformed in steps so that the result stands as an indexical record of the transformation, that is, as a text; in other words, the train wreck is always read from the train. Whatever their other limitations, blobs do something that neither formal typologies nor the train wreck can, which is to launch variation without origin.

In its coming theory, same will not be a mere aftereffect of difference; rather, the two will constitute independent coordinates in a context-dependent matrix. Same theory will parallel difference theory: if "différance," therefore, then "samenance." After all, in a scheme generalized for all meaning by Derrida, if two male antelopes are in the presence of a tiger, their sameness is more impor-

tant, though their difference is operative; if they are in the presence of a mating female, their difference is more important, though sameness also operates. Where to start? With Leibniz's monadology, I suggest, in which each monad is different yet the same in its difference, giving rise to the most variety with the greatest coherence. Or with Houellebecq's darkly optimistic anticipation of same theory in *Elementary Particles* (*Les Particules élémentaires*). Both of those thoughts, too, were leaps.

1. Deleuze has also written the same comic scene in *Le Pli,* in a Christian setting: "The totality would allow us to utter in the same breath, like Balthasar, 'Everything is ordinary!' and 'Everything is unique!'"

Scene from *The Life of Brian* by Monty Python

Peter Eisenman

The Affects of Disaster

Referring to the Ground Zero master plan competition recently, Rem Koolhaas used the phrase "an architect of disaster." While his phrase was laced with his customary irony, he nevertheless used the word *disaster* in its usual sense. For me, however, the events of September 11, 2001, and the literal disaster of the World Trade Center collapse suggest a different way to use the term.

The September 11, 2001, disaster was a media event, staged, it has been suggested, so that one half hour after the first plane hit the first tower, the entire world would witness on live television the second plane hitting the second tower. It was perhaps the last of the great spectacles, in the sense described by Guy Debord in 1967 in his book *The Society of the Spectacle*. What has been seen in the media since September 11, 2001, may mark the beginning of the end game of the society of the spectacle. Watching live coverage of the war in Iraq on CNN—the toxic-green images of men firing guns at one another at night—it is impossible to tell whether one is watching a computer game, a film, or reality. The contemporary proliferation of media has led to a confusion of reality and fiction, which is at the heart of the spectacle. This confusion has provoked a crisis of unity that all

language, and more specifically architecture, is facing: the loss of the differentiation between fact and fiction, between the thing and its representation.

This crisis between reality and its mediation is related to the difference between being there—being physically at a place, for example, feeling the terror on September 11 at the World Trade Center—and witnessing it, thousands of miles removed, on a video monitor in Tokyo, Capetown, or London. Being there has always been the domain of architecture. The media's blurring of reality therefore affects architecture, which historically has been thought to be the locus of reality and the repository of a metaphysics of presence. Today, the assumed truth of this metaphysics of presence is seen as a historical fiction, thus contributing to the metaphoric disaster that architecture faces.

In his book *The Writing of the Disaster*, Maurice Blanchot uses the term *disaster* to mean not the loss of the unity of language but rather the loss of the capacity of language to express the excesses of the events of Hiroshima, Auschwitz, Dresden, and others. In going beyond expression, these excesses deny language its former absolute nature.

Blanchot identifies two conditions of language that have been affected by this loss of the possibility of language to express the absolute. One is the language of expression; the other is the language of creation. The possibility of expression always assumes that language is a given within the tradition of a transcendental metaphysics. Expression assumes language to be capable of truth, authority, and an absolute value. The September 11, 2001, disaster alerted us to the exhaustion of our languages' ability to express and to represent. Thus disaster becomes a useful metaphor that allows us to question the larger problem of language, and more specifically architecture as the embodiment of a supposed metaphysics of presence.

The language of creation, on the other hand, is different from the language of expression in that it finds a creative potential within language. The difference between expression and creation is like the difference between Bernini and Borromini, as pointed out by Rudolf Wittkower. Bernini, he said, was the first architect to import theatrical effects from other disciplines; as a spectacle of effects, his buildings created subjective affects and a more passive observer. Borromini, on the other hand, explored architecture's internal capacity to produce originary spatial effects through the elision of complex geometric figures to generate new plastic forms. Borromini's work played upon affects in the work itself, affects that produced objective as opposed to subjective conditions. The creative thus involves what Jeffrey Kipnis calls "irreducible effects outside of the history of the metaphysics of presence," because it creates originary affects that are internal to architecture. The expressive, being wholly theatrical and subjective, does not produce such autonomous affects.

The opening produced by the disaster allows us to critique the metaphysics of presence as an illusion constructed in history. Expression is an effect of these illusions. Creation comes out of the essence of the discipline and is an affect produced outside of that history. This disruption of the former unity between expression and creation produces the possibility of something between the two—an opening up to a rigor coming from within architecture that no longer relies on the metaphysics of presence but instead leads to effects that are new and originary.

TOWARD GENETIC ARCHITECTURE

Karl Chu

Nothing signifies the end of the era of man—and with it, a certain anthropocentric conception of time, history, and architecture—more than the completion of the Human Genome Project, a self-referential index of man written in a language that is not unique to man. The project, which would not have been possible without the convergence of computation and biogenetics, symbolizes the power of instrumental reason in transforming the substance of physical reality into the domain of possible worlds. We are moving into a post-human era, when new forms of bio-machinic mutation of substances and values may lead architecture beyond the confines of anthropology. A neobiological civilization or other brave new worlds now loom over the horizon. The world that is emerging may be like a jungle in which multiple species, including protospecies of genetic architecture, coexist within a virtual ecology comprised of artificial life and abstract machines.

Even though architecture today is increasingly absorbed into the social, political, and economic realms, it has so far remained impervious to developments that are taking place within genetic engineering and the biotechnology industry. Two different architectural approaches have emerged within this context, which I characterize as "morphodynamical" and "morphogenetic" systems. One attempts to base form on external dynamics; the other generates form using internal genetic logics.

The morphodynamical orientation has taken two distinct directions: the first, exemplified by the work of Rem Koolhaas, inadvertently conceives architecture as the instrument of capitalism and, as a consequence, rarely interrogates the internal logic of its formal constitution. It relies on the default language of modern architecture to package and modulate the flow of complex programs based on external constraints such as infrastructure, statistics, density, branding, the global market economy, and so on. The second direction emphasizes so-called soft morphology and is represented by a host of young architects working in the digital domain with little or no awareness of the theoretical biases implicit in their work. These architects use interactive morphing models that are spuriously linked to external forces derived from the context. This strategy often confuses the difference between modeling and simulation. Both of these approaches tacitly appeal to concepts derived from dynamical systems and chaos theory, filtered through the conceptual logic of Gilles Deleuze and Félix Guattari. These outside-in methodologies rely on the logics of "flow" and "morphing" to give shape and form to architecture. Underlying these approaches is the assumption that architecture is primarily an adaptive discipline lacking autonomy; its reason for being is predicated on it being woven, critically or otherwise, into a given context of forces and relations.

The morphogenetic approach, which is based on the logic of an internal principle or code that generates morphology, seeks to establish the autonomy of architecture. It is related to Peter Eisenman's notion of interiority and autonomy of the generative. Whereas Eisenman's notion of interiority is derived from the historicity of architecture, the concept of interiority that I am proposing is based on genetics, which relies on an algorithmic logic of recursion. In general, genetic determination is inherently plural: interactions of autonomous agents or genotypes give rise to phenotypes or end morphologies. The process of genetic recursion has an autonomous, internal logic, which resists semiological regimes of meaning that refer to ready-made typologies. This strategy can be understood as an emancipatory move that exemplifies how architecture can be self-generating without degenerating into a self-indulgent pathology.

Architecture must explore its own generative capacity instead of relying on external narratives and symbolic appropriation to legitimize itself. At the beginning of the twenty-first century, the future of architecture is confronted with counterfactual possibilities that are waiting to be explored and brought into existence. The world is intrinsically genetic and generative in its propulsion toward possible futures; so is genetic architecture in its movement toward the construction of possible worlds.

Envelope + Public/Private

The envelope, or exterior skin of a building, is one of architecture's most fundamental components. The idea of the envelope as a boundary, something that separates a protected interior from an untamed exterior, is a persistent one, even as what is being segregated continues to change. One of the most important delineations drawn by building envelopes today is the one between the public and private spheres. These terms refer to a clouded and overlapping set of conditions—including access (open versus restricted), ownership (state versus individual), law (areas subject to state scrutiny versus those protected from disclosure), and social domains (commercial or governmental versus domestic)—which makes any attempt to define the public and private through architecture both loaded and complex. With the many recent innovations in building enclosures, from curved forms to high-tech structures to double envelopes, will architecture in the twenty-first century perform the separations between inside and outside, public and private, differently from its predecessors?

Bernard Tschumi observes that the envelope is invariably a site of social relationships—whether of conflict or pleasure. He demonstrates how envelopes, when integrated with program, movement, and context, can materialize concepts. Extending Tschumi's line of inquiry, K. Michael Hays theorizes how we might begin to understand the new envelopes in relation to their social context, which includes new construction technologies, the globalized market economy, and digital media.

Beatriz Colomina places architectural envelopes within a different context, tracing the influence on modern architecture of developments in medicine, particularly the invention of X rays and CAT scans. Citing the latest innovations in medical imaging techniques, she suggests new directions for how architects might approach buildings conceived as bodies.

Three prominent contemporary architects offer provocative examples of the new envelopes. Zaha Hadid's Wolfsburg Science Center, for instance, seamlessly integrates envelope, form, structure, and program while blurring the distinction between public and private space. Greg Lynn also uses seamlessness, but to different ends, in the design of a housing project in the Netherlands and also in an innovative tea set. Lynn is interested in utilizing advanced production technologies to explore the ways that envelopes can at once express identity and differentiation.

The terms *public* and *private* are given a fresh coloring in Rem Koolhaas's essay on his abiding passion for the skyscraper. From a boutique hotel in New York City to, most recently, the Central Chinese Television Headquarters in Beijing, Koolhaas explores the potential for the skyscraper and its envelope to function as a social interface.

Finally, Mark Rakatansky focuses on the role of the building envelope as a kind of map—a chart of the social and other dynamics at play in a work of architecture. He hints at how architecture might express these relationships in more complex and articulate ways.

VECTORS AND ENVELOPES

Bernard Tschumi

Buildings, in their simplest form, are made of vectors and envelopes. How one enters a building and moves through it constitutes the vectors. What keeps out the rain, cold, heat, noise, and burglars constitutes the envelope. Vectors activate; envelopes define.

Vectors typically are related to program. Envelopes usually respond to context, whether social, cultural, political, or geographic. Together, vectors, envelopes, programs, and contexts are the basic terms of the architectural equation—a simple proposition that centuries of art and architectural history somehow have obscured. Materials, of course, are another important factor: architecture is the materialization of ideas or concepts. But materials also can be understood as part of the sociocultural, political, or geographic context.

There is no architecture without vectors, envelopes, programs, and contexts. But there also is no architecture without a concept or an idea. Concept—not form, as some would suggest—is what distinguishes architecture from mere building.

What is an envelope, conceptually? I prefer the terms *envelope* or *enclosure* to *facade,* a word that connotes a host of compositional clichés. Yet like facades, enclosures are not free from sociocultural and geopolitical influences. Their chief function is to define boundaries, in particular, boundaries between the public and the private. In doing so, they establish relationships. For example, an enclosure can be sealed or porous, it can be a bastion or a veil, it can exclude or include. An envelope can abruptly

divide as well as subtly connect. Enclosures range from the militaristic to the erotic, from crude, fortified limits to subtle, psychological screens that suggest exhibitionism or voyeurism. Ultimately, the envelope is the delimitation of the social. It defines the spaces of conflict as much as the boundaries of pleasure.

New kinds of envelopes have been made possible by contemporary technologies. How do these articulate exclusion or inclusion? Is the enclosure real and material? Can it be virtual and immaterial? Is it a single layer or a composite of multiple superimposed membranes? How do apparently static envelopes relate to the dynamics of movement, the vectors within them?

The interaction between envelopes and vectors can be approached in several ways. It can be a relationship of indifference, reciprocity, or conflict. Indifference is the condition in which there is no relation between the envelope and what happens inside it. Reciprocity is like an ideal kitchen, in which everything is in exactly the right place to be reached by the most efficient bodily movements. Conflict is the situation in which everything is strategically in the wrong place—such as if one tried to play ice hockey in the living room.

The relationships of indifference, reciprocity, and conflict can also be applied to the interaction between concept and context. Selecting one of these relationships is a matter of architectural strategy.

For Lerner Hall, the student center at Columbia University, we designed a glass wall supported by a system of ramps to establish a direct connection between the envelope and the movement vectors. The relation between the ramps and the envelope is one of absolute reciprocity, yet this integration can give way to programmatic disjunction; for instance, a dance company used the ramps as a stage and the curtain wall as a screen for performances in a kind of dis-programming or cross-programming.

We explored a very different strategy in our Concert Hall and Exhibition Complex in Rouen, France. Designed to accommodate up to eight thousand people, the auditorium is used for popular music performances, political meetings, sporting events, and large trade fair exhibitions. The size of the project is staggering: it is one thousand feet long and two hundred feet wide. The most crucial, and expensive, part of the building is the enclosure. That is where the architecture begins. The building features a double envelope: one of concrete and the other of steel. The double envelope is designed to separate; it acts as a sound buffer between the inside of the auditorium, where the volume rises to 105 decibels during large rock con-

certs, and the outside, where only 35 decibels are permitted. Located between the respective logics of the two envelopes is a resulting space. This "in-between" becomes the social space, the site of meetings and interactions, activated by the movement of crowds on ramps or stairs.

The translation of concepts into built reality is a complex process. A photograph of the building under construction before the application of the cladding looks like an X ray: the movement vectors, the interior concrete skin, and the arches of the steel skeleton are all visible. The shell-like form gives the structure strength and allows long spans to be covered with extremely light latticework framing without diagonal bracing. Superimposed onto this are layers of water barriers, insulation, and metal. The envelope therefore is not homogeneous but is comprised of a series of layers. It appears as a perfect, detailed envelope but is actually a heterogeneous composite. As is often the case in architecture, the surface belies greater complexities. Here, the surface defines a space that in turn accommodates and intensifies the social.

Concert Hall and Exhibition Complex, Rouen, France, 2001

THE ENVELOPE AS MEDIATOR

K. Michael Hays

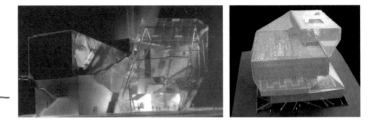

The emblematic significance of the new envelope lies in the immediacy of the envelope to the social world—that is, in the envelope's determinate relation to advanced design technologies, high-end construction technologies, to money and financing, property and real estate, to what we usually call the forces and relations of production. At the same time, it is reductive to say that the new envelopes are mere representations of a particular stage of capital without giving some specificity and autonomy to architecture, a discipline and practice governed by its own internal dynamics and histories.

At a conference on the avant-garde in America held at Columbia University and the Museum of Modern Art in 1996, I proposed that one way to handle this theoretical problem in late modern buildings, or at least in the particular case of Mies van der Rohe's Seagram Building, was to introduce a set of mediating terms between the strictly architectural and the strictly social, as it were. One term is an internal, discipline-specific, architectural, and constructional one: the curtain wall woven out of the famous I-section and glass and steel panels, emblems of rationalization and standardization raised to art, the nexus of meaning of the entire building in all its functional, factural, and symbolic dimensions. The other term is one of external mediation: the logic of surface perception as given by the emergent consumerist culture of the late 1950s and early 1960s, whose subjects were being trained on mass advertising in magazines, billboards, and of course, television—the television screen, along with the computer screen with which it will eventually merge, being the ultimate surface toward which all others will gravitate. The abstraction of Mies's envelope, I argued, can be seen as both a reproduction of and a defense against this new logic of surface perception and the consumer-communication economy that sponsored it, an abstraction and a deterritorialization in architecture that is an analog of the abstraction and deterritorialization in society.[1]

Certainly some sort of media term is still the appropriate one to begin with when trying to understand how the new envelopes of our own time relate to their social ground, though of course that relationship will be different from the older modernist ones. What I suggest is that while the mediation of the modernist envelope was one of abstraction and negation, the mediation of the new envelope is rather more a process of smoothing and de-differentiation—a de-differentiation of form, technique, and experience, a spreading out so complete that the experience of the architectural envelope is no longer distinctive but is now part of an aesthetic experience that is diffused through and saturates every part of our lives and seems always and everywhere the same.

I have a few observations about the new envelope. First, it is perhaps obvious but still important to observe that the new envelopes are integrally tied to contemporary digital design technologies and specific kinds of software (Maya and CATIA, for example) that coordinate and synthesize multiple parameters and all sorts of data into a smooth, frictionless flow. An important feature of these design technologies is that their procedures and techniques are the generic ones of design, not specific to architecture, and can be applied to Audi TTs, iMacs, and animated films like *Shrek* as much as to buildings. It is consistent that the reception of the architecture thus produced will be woven into the same general media fabric as video games and televisual leisure, part of the smooth media mix.

Second, the notion of surface is still important for the new envelope, and this is evidence that it builds on the accumulated techniques and effects of early design models like Mies's curtain wall. But while in Mies's case, as with modernism generally, there was an isomorphism, a continuity of conception between the envelope and the space and structure that it enclosed, the new envelope is often detached from any support, developing under its own momentum, raised to a second power of the sort that the notion of simulacrum was reintroduced to name. In this way, the new envelope is also related to Venturi and Scott Brown's surface of the decorated shed. It is as if the surface of the modern envelope, which already traced the forces of reification and commodification in its very abstraction, has been further neutralized, reappropriated, and then attenuated and animated at a higher level. This new enveloping surface no longer corresponds to a particular social public or locale—neither Park Avenue nor Las Vegas nor Levittown—which is perhaps what gives it its slightly unreal quality, even when built.

The new surface is not made up of semiotic material appropriated from popular culture (as with Venturi and Scott Brown) but, nevertheless, is often modulated through procedures that trace certain external programmatic, sociological, or technological facts (what designers refer to as "datascapes"). These traces both articulate and animate the surface, implying differentiated possibilities for occupation, and encode phenomena outside the object that cannot, in their very nature, be represented directly, including a range of institutional, legal, technical, and cultural arrangements that precede, determine, and exist beyond the architectural object.

Third, the unprecedented degree of autonomy achieved by the new envelope does not operate to distinguish inside from outside or private from public but rather to effectively remove the possibility of making those distinctions. In the early, undeveloped versions, it seemed as if the envelope was just the surface of some gelatinous fluid, hence the name "blob." Sometimes in later versions, the envelope seems to function as what we used to call a datum or ground against which to read other parts of the building, or as a wrapper that holds together otherwise divergent parts of the building. But it is more often the case that the other parts of the building and the envelope all float at a distance from each other in a state of suspension, as if in some solution that has dissolved older distinctions, such as figure and ground, inside and out, or private and public. The envelope is in this sense deterritorialized far beyond even the abstraction of Mies. What is

more, it is this same deterritorialization, lack of meaning, and flattened-out neutrality that allows the envelope to be used as an axiomatic wrapper or membrane and to collapse programs and events that would otherwise seem impossibly unrelated.

The new envelope is a smoothed-out, neutralized, but animated surface. What remains for us to try to characterize is what I have called the external term of mediation, which would allow us to develop a triangulation that includes the social ground (which is unrepresentable) and the architectural figure of the envelope (the internal mediation) and thus to complete the theorization of the envelope as a representational figure. What is the nexus in our perceptual and conceptual decoding apparatus that would allow us to frame the experience of the unrepresentable real of present posturbanism and media technology similarly to the way that the curtain wall transcodes an earlier moment of advertising media and consumer society?

I have already established that this term or frame will surely also involve media, but now I want to be more specific. While it is too early to be certain about any external term of mediation, I suggest that one possibility to work on and modulate is something like what Raymond Williams in 1974 called "total flow": the constant emission of generic but continually changing bits of information that we move in and out of in a kind of ultimate suture between time and space.

It is true that total flow has its roots in the pop culture and media experience of a moment just before our present, but today the experience of the space-time of total flow is volatilized and then neutralized far beyond anything that architecture in the 1970s was able to accomplish. The emissions from video and computer screens neutralize psychic energy and homogenize experience into a kind of all-pervasive liquid force in such a way as to make total flow a

logical candidate with which to theorize the newer work in question. What is more, the deregulation of television or, at least, the possibility of "surfing" across hundreds of channels whose broadcasts never stop, is a suitable analog not only for the sort of spontaneous occupation desired by recent architecture but also for its complex economic ties to multinational capital and entertainment technologies.

A further advantage of the notion of total flow is that it has as its distant relative nothing less than distraction, which Walter Benjamin saw as the modern architectural mode of perception par excellence. This idea seems to be an adequate, preliminary conceptualization of aesthetic experience in our own time, when the de-differentiation of disciplines and the tendentious erasure of boundaries between specific cultural materials and practices promise to homogenize all distinction, difference, and otherness into a globalized, neutralized sameness, a randomized, spread-out delirium.

The new envelope analogously weakens disciplinary autonomy, de-differentiates procedures of design and dissemination, and attempts to dissolve the very distinction between the architectural representation and the larger world of image-spectacles. But the new envelope paradoxically (or dialectically) produces a link between the aesthetic experiences that it enables and the current abstract global system; the link is made as a triangulation of social space, architecture, and a historically specific media concept that frames the relationship between the two.

1. See my "Abstraction's Appearance (Seagram Building)," in *Autonomy and Ideology: Positioning an Avant-Garde in America*, ed. R. E. Somol (New York: The Monacelli Press, 1997).

From left: Mies van der Rohe, Seagram Building; Robert Venturi, Denise Scott Brown, and Steven Izenour, illustration from *Leaving Las Vegas*; Coop Himmelb(l)au, model of the UFA Cinema Center; Office for Metropolitan Architecture, model of the Seattle Public Library

Skinless Architecture

Beatriz Colomina

From top: Ludwig Mies van der Rohe, Glass Skyscraper, Berlin, Germany, 1922; M2A camera

The line between public and private no longer coincides with the outer limit of a building. We might even argue that the envelope is no longer to be found on the outside but instead has coiled itself up within an imaginary body.

Architectural envelopes respond more to our image of the human body than to functional programs. This is an old story. Architecture has always followed medicine. During the Renaissance, for example, when doctors investigated the mysterious interior of the body by cutting into and dissecting it, architects tried to understand the interior of the building by slicing section cuts through it. In the sketchbooks of Leonardo da Vinci, cutaway views of architectural interiors appeared beside anatomical drawings. He understood the interiors of the brain and womb in architectural terms, as enclosures that must be cut through to reveal their secrets. The central reference for architecture was no longer a whole body but a dissected, fragmented, analyzed body.

As medical representations changed so did architectural representations. In the twentieth century, for instance, the widespread use of X rays made a new way of thinking about architecture possible. If architectural discourse has from its beginning associated building and body, the body that it describes is the medical body, reconstructed by each new theory of health.

Modern architecture, for example, is unthinkable outside tuberculosis. The principles of modern architecture seem to have been taken straight out of medical texts on the disease, one of which in the late nineteenth century gave as causes of TB: "unfavorable climate, sedentary indoor life, defective ventilation and deficiency of light." In response, modern architects offered sun, light, ventilation, exercise, roof terraces, hygiene, and whiteness as means to prevent, if not cure, tuberculosis.

In his book *The Radiant City* of 1935, Le Corbusier dismissed the "natural ground" as a "dispenser of rheumatism and tuberculosis" and declared it to be "the enemy of man." He advocated pilotis to detach buildings from the "wet, humid ground where disease breeds" and roof gardens for sunbathing and exercise. He utilized medical pictures of the lungs and their inner workings as architectural illustrations and developed a concept of "exact respiration" whereby the indoor air was continually circulated and cleaned, made "dust free, disinfected, . . . and ready to be consumed by the lung." One by one, all the characteristic features of modern architecture (pilotis, roof garden, glass walls, and clean air) turn out to be medical devices.

Modern buildings even started to look like medical images. Mies van der Rohe described his Glass Skyscraper of 1922 as skin-and-bones architecture and rendered it as if seen through an X-ray machine. Mies was not alone. Architectural slide libraries are filled with images of translucent glass skins that reveal inner bones and organs. Take for example, Le Corbusier's Glass Skyscraper (1925), Walter Gropius's Bauhaus (1926), Brinkman and Van der Vlugt's Van Nelle factory in Rotterdam (1925–27), George Keck's Crystal House in the 1933–34 World's Fair in Chicago, and Paul Nelson's Suspended House (1935). This is more than a dominant aesthetic. It is a symptom of the deep influence of medical discourse on architecture.

X-ray technology and modern architecture were born around the same time and evolved in parallel. By midcentury, the see-through house had become a mass phenomenon, just as the mobilization against TB launched programs for the mass X-

INSIDE THE M2A™ CAPSULE

1. Optical dome
2. Lens holder
3. Lens
4. Illuminating LEDs (Light Emitting Diode)
5. CMOS (Complementary Metal Oxide Semiconductor) imager
6. Battery
7. ASIC (Application Specific Integrated Circuit) transmitter
8. Antenna

raying of entire populations. While the X ray exposed the inside of the body to the public eye, the modern building unveiled its interior, subjecting what was previously private to public scrutiny. In an interview published in *House Beautiful*, Edith Farnsworth, a successful Chicago doctor, compared her famous weekend house, designed by Mies van der Rohe in 1949, to an X ray, and cited a local rumor that the house was a tuberculosis sanatorium. The X-ray aesthetic was inseparable from the discourse about the disease.

The X ray is not simply an image of the body, however. More crucially, it is an image of the body being imaged. The X ray is not just about showing an inside. The exterior envelope remains as a kind of shadow or blur. To look at an X ray is to feel one's eye penetrating the surface of the body and moving through space. The very act of looking is exposed. It is inevitably voyeuristic. Perhaps that was what attracted architects to X rays from the beginning. With Mies, the glass is never completely transparent. Even at night one senses the outer limit of the building and one's eye passing through that limit. Modern architecture exposes itself, but not by revealing everything. Rather, it stages the act of exposure, calling the eye in.

At the turn of the twenty-first century, the CAT scan (Computerized Axial Tomography) may be for us what the basic X ray was for architects early in the twentieth century. In fact, the CAT scan is simply many X-ray images compiled by a computer to generate cross-sectional views and three-dimensional images of the body's internal organs. A typical medical brochure describes it thus: "Imagine the body as a loaf of bread and you are looking at one end of the loaf. As you remove each slice of bread, you can see the entire surface of that slice from the crust to the center." The crust, skin, or envelope

becomes an almost invisible line. What matters is the dense interior, which is rendered like a new, more complex kind of facade.

As with the X ray, architects have been quick to respond to the new technology. If architectural publications at the beginning and middle of the century were full of X rays, contemporary architectural publications are full of CAT-scan images. For example, in a 1992 catalog of an exhibition of his work, Josep Lluís Mateo shows a CAT scan of a brain on the cover and insists inside that "The architect has to act with the callousness of the medic: he cuts, analyses, researches. But he must never mummify an organism that lived once." Likewise, UN Studio shows CAT scans of the brain alongside projects in the firm's 1999 book *Move*. The Renaissance obsession with the brain continues into the twenty-first century, as does interest in the fetus—as evidenced by the "embryological" work being done by digital architects.

The influence of the CAT scan is reflected in recent architectural envelopes. In the Office for Metropolitan Architecture's Bibliothèque Nationale competition entry, the exposure of a skeleton behind a glass skin gives way to translucent bodies revealing organs. And Foreign Office Architects' Yokohama Port Terminal also seems to follow the logic of the CAT scan: an endless series of section cuts is used to assemble a three-dimensional body. At Yokohama, there is no simple opposition between the outside and the inside. The building aspires to be a continuously folded surface where structure and skin are one, and where there are no bones or discrete organs.

Today, there are new instruments of medical diagnosis, new systems of representation. So if we want to talk about the state of the art in building

envelopes, we should look to the very latest techniques of imaging the body and ask ourselves what effects they may have on the way we conceive buildings.

The latest techniques represent yet another radical transformation of our thinking regarding the relationship between inside and outside. For example, the M2A camera that was approved by the FDA in 2001 is a one-inch-long disposable camera that is swallowed as a pill. M2A is short for "mouth to anus." It snaps two color pictures per second for eight hours as it passes through the twenty-two-foot-long digestive tract. A recorder the size of a Walkman collects 57,000 color images while a person goes about normal business. The images are then downloaded on a computer to produce a video of the camera's journey.

Like the 1966 movie *Fantastic Voyage*, in which a team of scientists is shrunk and injected into the body to repair a brain injury, the M2A transforms the body into an occupiable interior. The body is turned inside out, making the skin irrelevant. All that remains is an endless interior, bathed in the light from the capsule video camera. The capsule itself looks like a hybrid of the buildings inspired by X rays and CAT scans. A translucent envelope exposes the outlines of the inner mechanisms while a transparent head serves as the viewing apparatus. This hybrid displaces both the transparent and translucent systems in favor of a skinless body, one no longer even experienced as a body. The architectural analog would be the skinless building, the building turned inside out to such an extent that it may not be clear it is a building. What exactly this complete loss of the envelope means for architecture is unclear, but in an age in which the public/private distinction is so radically dissolved, an architecture without envelopes may well be upon us.

MOVEMENT AND POROSITY

In thinking about the role of the building envelope in separating public and private, the notion of the boundary is critical. One idea that I have been exploring in recent projects is porosity: drawing public space into a building's interior to make a series of public rooms in the city. This is partly a response to living in London, where the buildings tend to be fortified and public spaces come about by accident rather than by design. Porosity suggests a new kind of urbanism, composed of streams or flows of movement that cut through the city fabric.

In our Science Center in Wolfsburg, Germany, for instance, multiple threads of pedestrian and vehicular movement are pulled through an artificial landscape and into the building, creating intersecting paths of movement. The building is structured in such a way that it maintains a large degree of transparency and porosity on the ground level. The main volume, the exhibition space, is raised over an outdoor public plaza. The continuous platform of the museum is supported by a series of concrete cones that on the ground level are smaller in scale and at the top open up to accommodate the museum programs. These large craters form a family of spaces, a continuous landscape in which the distinctions between skin and structure, public and private, are eroded. The ambiguity of the building envelope presents visitors with a degree of complexity and strangeness, intended to give rise to curiosity and discovery.

Science Center, Wolfsburg, Germany, 2000–2003

Greg Lynn

Calculated Variations

Despite the fact that calculus is more than three hundred years old, the advent of the computer allows us to be among the first architects and designers to work intuitively with a new class of shapes that are calculus-based—that is, built out of interconnected and interacting variables. Besides being marked by variegation, undulation, and rhythmic change, envelopes described with calculus have a high degree of continuity. This combination of variability and continuity yields a quality I call "intricacy," meaning that the parts communicate with the whole to achieve a synthesis or holism. Visually, intricate forms have an organic quality, but this does not mean that they have been grown or that they are natural. Intricately organic forms cannot simply be abstracted from natural models or shaped to mimic natural forms. The only way to generate intricacy is to work with the rigors and proportions derived from calculus.

The topological surfaces that characterize contemporary calculus-based design are meshes made from networks of curves, or separatrices. This term was popularized in architecture by Jeffrey Kipnis fifteen years ago in his essay "/Twisting the Separatrix/." The word *separatrix* is borrowed from Jacques Derrida, but is also invoked in a different spatial and formal manner by Gilles Deleuze. Its definition is simple: a separatrix is a curve, even if straight, that both unites and divides two disparate systems. In several of my office's recent projects ranging from Dutch public housing to Italian teapots, I have revived the idea of separatrices and followed the continuities and differential variations that they make possible as they engage different social, material, and contextual issues.

In approaching the design of a public housing project south of Amsterdam, for example, I explicitly avoided making an argument that an intricate form is the best form for social collectivity. Nonetheless, the forms used are directly linked to a new type of social organization as well as to a new image for the building. The developers of the housing project planned to renovate an existing building to include 250 units offered to buyers and 250 subsidized units offered to renters. I wanted to break the architectural monotony and the social segregation between the demographic groups that would occupy the different units and to give identity to these various groups. We therefore proposed defining discrete "neighborhoods" of ten units, each with its own position in the nearly kilometer-long block and each with a unique shape and organization. In order to achieve this diversity of position

and configuration, we introduced thirteen escalators; these are clipped onto the existing building with a series of eleven-story vertical trusses that expand in girth wherever they are needed to support a load. The intricacies of this project emerge with the repetition of these new vertical trusses. For both structural and aesthetic reasons, we have written custom software with Bentley Systems that allows us to adjust the smoothing of the shapes vertically and horizontally based on the load points of each escalator. Like drops of water on a surface, these forces interact and ripple across the facade, creating a complex and continuous yet differentiated pattern across the elements. Each of the 154 trusses is a super-component that is welded, assembled, galvanized, painted, and clad in the factory, then shipped on a boat to the site and picked up in one giant section.

Concurrent with the Amsterdam housing project, we designed a coffee and tea set for Alessi. I had an idea that by using some deregulated aircraft technology for forming metal, we could make ensembles of teapots and ship them in the molds in which they were made. We drew up a family of curves that were compatible when surfaced together, put those into a spreadsheet program, and generated fifty thousand variations of the coffee pot. We found a way to manufacture them by heating aerospace-grade titanium to nine hundred degrees until it became soft, using an oven depressurized to have the same atmosphere as outer space. The titanium is then inflated into a CNC (computer numerically controlled) machined carbon mold by igniting argon gas between two welded sheets.

The graphitelike CNC forms cost less than $1,000 to tool, whereas in stamped stainless steel, they would cost upward of $200,000. So for a $1,000 premium you can create mass-produced art, allowing everybody to have a one-of-a-kind object.

For me, the key theoretical and formal issue was how to design an edition of fifty thousand unique objects that had identity in their variation. The most banal effect of CAD (computer-aided design) and CNC technologies is yet more variety, which is the worst quality with which I can imagine being associated. Variety is just anything goes; variation is organization and structure at multiple levels of interconnected hierarchical order. One theory of variation is intricacy, where elements are related and connected to their neighboring elements in a continuous undulating series that is determined by both a generic limit of the elements and by a holistic organization of their interaction. There is both holism and discreteness to each component in the Alessi sets and to the sets as a collection. Intricate qualities result when elements retain their individuation while entraining one another, producing larger-scale organizations that are connected continuously to finer, microscopic scales of organization. Once this principle of calculus is understood and incorporated by architects, the potential of the new tools of digital design will be realized.

From left: Coffee and Tea Piazza for Alessi, 2003; transformation of the Kleiburg housing block in the Bijlmermeer, the Netherlands, 2005

Rem Koolhaas

SKYSCRAPER: A TYPOLOGY OF PUBLIC AND PRIVATE

The year 1972 saw the planting of a number of seeds that came to fruition roughly thirty years later in a totally unpredictable manner. It was the year that the World Trade Center opened, perhaps representing the maximum modernity that Americans were capable of producing at that moment. The year 1972 was also the year that I arrived in New York, a city that was universally disliked at the time by the thinking sides of the architectural establishments of both Europe and America. I remember a series of contentious and unpleasant conversations in which people tried to cure me of my continuing interest not only in New York but particularly in the World Trade Center. At that time, the Twin Towers were regarded by the architectural elite of New York as the absolute pit of antiurban nonarchitecture.

Also in 1972, Robert Venturi and Denise Scott Brown published *Learning from Las Vegas,* a book that prompted a new direction in architecture, leading to such works as Philip Johnson's AT&T Building and Michael Graves's proposed extension to the Whitney Museum of American Art. Subsequently, nearly all of the architecture realized in Manhattan was derived from these two models, which disregarded program in favor of a theoretical contextuality and a relentless pursuit of form. That it is no longer imaginable that serious architects would present buildings like these indicates that maybe there is progress. In the 1970s, the popular interpretation of urbanism was also quite primitive: urbanism was "streets," and although New York had many streets, any manipulation of the existing street pattern was seen as wrong.

That seemed to change in 1998 when our office was asked by Ian Schrager to design a boutique hotel, along with Herzog & de Meuron. We saw an opportunity to resuscitate the World Trade Center idea and initially proposed to fill the site of the hotel, Astor Place in New York City, with a proliferation of miniature Twin Towers. Although Schrager was enthusiastic at first, he became increasingly uncomfortable with our scheme. Thirty years after its construction, the World Trade Center remained a reviled object, even in a miniaturized and beautiful version. After going through five or six versions, we finally settled on what was perhaps the most radically different thing one could imagine from the Twin Towers: a huge rock, perforated with holes or grottoes, that floated above Astor Place. From a modernist monolith, we went to the other extreme of the most atavistic monument possible. Foreshadowing events yet to come, one could say we went from the World Trade Center to the caves of Tora Bora in Afghanistan.

Our project was canceled, but we continue to be fascinated by the typology of the skyscraper, with its potential to combine an endless series of unpredictable activities into social adventures. It is one of those weird typologies that was almost perfect at the moment of its invention but subsequently has regressed. The height of the high-rise is not interesting to us; instead, it is the coexistence of different entities within a single building that remains fascinating.

We decided that before we could do anything else we had to turn away from looking introvertedly at architecture to thinking about the wide range of different forms of intelligence that are necessary for architecture, including representation, politics, sociology, and anthropology. This led us to think about the regime of "¥€$," a term that describes the apparent apotheosis and idolatry of the market economy. We also considered a concept that I call "junk space," which is related to the spectacularization of contemporary space. The purpose of these investigations was not to abandon architecture but, on the contrary, to mobilize architecture as a way of organizing and looking at the world, creating coherence, rethinking representation, and extending the idea of planning to have a political effect.

The appearance of the ¥€$ regime and junk space, and the transformation of the city from a public to an increasingly private space, led us to redirect our view to Europe and to Asia. We are working now on a project in China, a country that is still, whatever people say, Communist. It is Communist not in the form of Maoist slogans but in the form of the state and, particularly, a state that can still have a project. In America and Europe, the state no longer has a project, and this has led to a shrinking role for architects, as it is increasingly difficult for us to align ourselves with an enterprise for the public good.

China is at an interesting moment of transition. The conventional view has always been that China and communism would collapse under the weight of their contradictions. Today, the mood is quite different. The government is changing and a new generation adamant about making China a modern state are taking positions of responsibility. This generation grew up during the Cultural

Revolution, saw the opening up of the country under Deng Xiaoping, and are leading the current expansion outward. Living through three such radical experiences generates a certain kind of intelligence.

China attracts endless carpetbaggers, no area more than the new central business district planned for the east side of the Forbidden City. On the whole, the work of Western and foreign architects in China is incredibly cynical and insulting, aimed toward the assumed vulgarity of Chinese culture. This situation will change drastically, not only because of the sophistication of the Chinese but also through the influence of external forces such as the 2008 Olympics in Beijing.

One of the things that will be a key in the articulation of a new China will be the headquarters of the Chinese national television corporation, CCTV, which is expanding on an almost unimaginable scale for the 2008 Olympics. The Chinese government asked us to design a building for CCTV that is 5.5 million square feet. The building does not consist of a headquarters that is separated from a studio complex in the cheaper part of the city, with scriptwriters in the funky part of town. It contains the entire program of television in the most expensive area of the city: a condition possible only under communism. The building is organized not as a tower but as a single integrated loop chaining together all the elements of the program: production, studios, media, and administration. The essence of the building is to take the high out of high-rise and to redirect the evolution of the tower to its potential for a social interface.

To this end, we are developing emblems or symbols that will be placed on the building facade. We are exploring iconographies that will be appropriate for this complex moment and context, and that will give the building a political charge.

The entire building is wrapped in an irregular grid that is denser where it needs to work harder—that is, carry more stress. We are developing the structure with Cecil Balmond. One of the things we are considering now is how the project should look. Beijing is either very dusty, with only silhouettes visible, or crystal clear, with only surfaces visible. The only tangible presences are buildings under construction. We are looking for something similar: a new kind of transparent cladding that is better than glass, with the structure represented as a kind of cutout or void.

We had a Chinese rendering company create a computer perspective that has a beautiful quality unachievable by Europeans alone or by Chinese alone. In that sense, it reminds me of the United Nations building, a building that an American could never have thought of, but a European could never have built. What we want is some of the same complexity of collaboration.

Coincidentally, the summer that we were working on this project, architecture by Americans in China started to become unpopular. The apparently god-given right of certain U.S. corporate design firms to despoil large sections of Asia seemed to be coming to a halt. At the same time, it was the summer of the Enron collapse and other scandals on Wall Street. So what had seemed to be a vigorous and honest system that could insist that the Chinese needed to reform and to "get with the program" began itself to look increasingly like a dream.

CCTV Tower, Beijing, China, 2002

ENVELOPE PLEASE

Mark Rakatansky

Let's say that the building envelope is a kind of map, that it maps the dialogues between insides and outsides, inclusions and exclusions, programs and contexts. The question is not just what might be mapped in and by the envelope, but whether the envelope shows itself to be in the act of mapping, in the act of performing various kinds of envelopings. In order to be performative, at the very least, a dialogue is necessary. Characters only emerge through their reactions and responses to other characters and situations, which is why the best monologues, tragic or comic, are always dialogues with the others in the self. It is through this simultaneous collapse and separation, continuity and collision, that the differential characteristics of characters are drawn forth.

Mappings therefore need to respond to—to dialogue with—other mappings in order to draw forth the character of their mapping. We all know how hard it is to map even one thing rigorously, but no thing means anything unless it's in relation to something else. As Bateson said, it doesn't take one to know one, it takes two to know one. In fact, I would say, if it takes two to know one, then really it takes three to tango. Three is the minimum number—if you want to get beyond simple binary juxtapositions into more complex and poignant relations.

You can know this like you know the back of your own hand if you just take a look at the back of your hand to see how the collages of veins, muscles, tendons, bones, joints, ligaments, nerves, and nails appear as inflective and inflected systems, emerging and disappearing, coincident and noncoincident. All of this brings complex differential articulations to the enveloping that is the skin.

Imagine structural, infrastructural, programmatic, typological, ideological, informational, material mappings appearing in architecture as inflective and inflected systems, emerging and disappearing, coincident and noncoincident—what an architecture that would be! It is through the tracking of how each of these mappings inflects and influences the others that these performances become interesting: neither collapsing into each other nor remaining entirely separate—cross-indexing and cross-determining while remaining legibly vivid and evocative.

Architects could thus be playing with the coincidence and noncoincidence of the envelope to the various and varying public and private attributes of site, program, iconography, structure, and material. Coincidence in both senses of the word: correlation and happenstance, codetermination and redetermination.

Thus rather than deciding whether our buildings are supposed to be either open or closed, inside-out or outside-in, attentive or distracted, public or private, we can let them be on the verge of, in the midst of, thinking out loud about their decisions—allow our buildings to perform their differential decisioning, their differential enveloping.

So let's open up the envelope but not announce the winner just yet. Or if we announce this year's winner, know that there will be another winning envelope next year, and the year after that. Let's open up the envelope and pull outside what's in, but let's leave it with that look of anticipation, that look of being on the verge, like Bernini's sculptures where the lips are parted in the midst of speaking.

Globalization + Criticism

The pairing of globalization and criticism might appear lopsided and odd at the beginning of the twenty-first century. After all, globalization is ubiquitous, inexorable, and ascendant, whereas criticism, by most accounts, is ineffectual, disappearing, and on the retreat. Globalization is the high school quarterback, and criticism is the pimple-faced geek. Globalization is advancing and nothing can stop it—criticism least of all. This is the conventional wisdom, at any rate. But the match-up may be the most important one of the century, and the results are bound to affect architecture.

Joan Ockman provides a lucid overview, defining the terms of the debate, and debunking the idea that the fight is already over and that we are now in a "postcritical" era. Instead, she asks what kind of criticism can exist in an age of globalization. One possible direction is suggested by Mark C. Taylor, who argues that globalization itself gives rise to a new kind of structure—complex adaptive systems (such as the Internet or global financial markets) that require novel critical and theoretical models. Architects and architecture critics might have a role to play in developing and understanding the network structures of these new systems.

Likewise, Saskia Sassen points to an opening for criticism and architecture in the new global landscape. Observing that globalization disrupts existing orders and makes visible previously unseen populations and linkages, she urges architects to search for forms—architectural and otherwise—of globality that extend beyond those currently available.

Offering his own disruptive form of globality is the architect Colin Fournier, who recently has been a key actor in the implantation of a "friendly alien" in Graz, Austria, in the form of a new art museum. It is, he observes, a building that could not have been built in England, where his practice is based, providing evidence for his claim that globalization can be a catalyst for urban innovation.

Although equally international in the scope of his practice, Enrique Norten puts aside the label "global architect," instead posing a series of questions about just what constitutes a global architecture. Isn't all architecture, he argues, site-specific? Terence Riley adopts a related position, raising a skeptical eyebrow at the pervasiveness of the global and arguing for architecture's rootedness in specific places. Criticism, too, he argues, is most effective when it is local.

Gwendolyn Wright and Yehuda Safran both focus on the language of globalization. Wright decodes some of the terms frequently used in architectural forums in relation to globalization and urges architects to reexamine long-held assumptions, while Safran suggests that a community of shared architectural language can link architects across national borders.

Joan Ockman

Criticism in the Age of Globalization

What is the relationship between globalization and criticism? At the beginning of the twenty-first century, globalization appears to be a keyword, and increasingly a buzzword and a code word for a dominant new set of relations of production. It is also one of the major processes or phenomena associated with what has come to be called postmodernity. The idea of criticism or critical judgment, on the other hand, goes back to the Enlightenment, has deep roots in the Marxist tradition, and belongs to the mindset we associate with modernity.

As such, it has been suggested that we are now living in a "post-critical" age. It is true that global restructuring has ushered in unprecedented forces of temporal and spatial compression, reducing distances and speeding up time, both of which—distance and time—seemed necessary in the past for genuine critical reflection. It has also given us a pervasive sense of

cultural relativism, making us aware that there is no longer any Archimedean point, any privileged position, from which to do criticism. Finally, what Fredric Jameson has spoken of as the becoming economic of the cultural and the becoming cultural of the economic—in other words, the market's contamination of every sphere of life, including the intellectual—has cast doubts on the possibility of preserving any really objective or autonomous domain for critical practice. Together, all these developments suggest an antithetical or antagonistic relationship between globalization and criticism.

So my first impulse is to ask: can there be criticism in an age of globalization? But because I remain suspicious of the glibness of formulations like the postcritical, which in the end are cynical inasmuch as they leave the dominant system unchallenged, if not strongly reinforced, the ques-

tion I wish to put on the table is rather: what kind of criticism can there be in an age of globalization?

A few more words about globalization. First, it is imperative to deconstruct the familiar binary opposition of global/local. Anyone who has CNN or Al Jazeera beaming into their bedroom right now can attest to the fact that everything local is thoroughly permeated by the global, and everything global ultimately becomes inflected by the local. The interdependence of these two asymmetrical force fields makes for all sorts of hybrid, syncretic, and frequently paradoxical effects. In his book *Modernity at Large,* Arjun Appadurai rejects the notion that globalization is a juggernaut transforming the world into a monoculture, invoking the concept of indigenization to describe the complex and fluid ways global phenomena—among them, what he calls mediascapes, technoscapes, financescapes, ethnoscapes, and ideoscapes—

infiltrate the imagination of contemporary citizens and become annexed and absorbed in local situations. The Guggenheim Museum in Bilbao is a stunning example of a building by an American superstar that was commissioned by the municipal authorities of a fiercely independent region in Spain; it has not only put the city on the international tourist map but effectively regenerated the local economy and revitalized the city's historical culture. Gehry's titanium and glass building looks like an object from another world, but it has also served to make Bilbao "appear" again, poignantly evoking the city's past as a center of industrial production through both its own metallic presence and the shock of its postindustrial "otherness."

More generally with respect to architecture and its criticism, it is not just the media that has a global reach today. Architectural practice has become thoroughly globalized, as has architectural education. Even architectural experience cannot exactly be said to be local, at least psychologically. As Dean MacCannell has suggested in his book *The Tourist,* and as the firm of Diller + Scofidio dramatizes, the sense of always being a tourist may be inherent to postmodern identity. Outside of our most intimate living environment, we tend to experience the contemporary world as strangers or at best as guests, and even that which we call home can be very *unheimlich* when it happens to be a hotel or a refugee camp.

Second, the term *globalization* is, as has already been suggested, multivalent and far from innocent, and in discussing it, it is necessary to keep in mind what purposes it serves, how it is mobilized, and what its effects are—in other words, to think critically about it. Globalization variously signifies the hegemony of a worldwide capitalist system on the economic plane; the superseding of the primacy of the nation-state by transnational arrangements, both formal and informal, on the political one; the emergence of new, networked information and communication instrumentalities on the technological one; and the advent of an increasingly homogeneous, consumer-oriented lifestyle and mentality on the cultural one. This last, which often comes under the rubric of postmodernism, first emerged as a new consciousness in the 1960s with McLuhan's annunciation of the global village, Debord's diatribe against a society of spectacle, and such "proto-global" architectural projects as Archigram's Walking City and Instant City or Superstudio's Continuous Monument.

In any event, globalization since the end of the cold war has quickly also become a code word for westernization, Americanization, and the neo-imperial ambitions of the United States. As such, from a traditional leftist point of view, it has been criticized for its suppression of difference, eradication of local traditions and heritages, environmental depredation, subjugation of poor people, and economic privatization and deregulation. These last have been accused of leading to wild forms of capitalism, transnational criminal networks, and finally global terrorism. In recent years, in places like Seattle, Genoa, and Pôrto Alegre, an antiglobalization movement has mobilized around various of these issues.

Within architecture, Kenneth Frampton's theory of critical regionalism, self-described as a rearguard position and initially articulated in the 1980s, has been the most highly elaborated stand against the inroads of cultural uniformity and environmental exploitation.

At the same time, from a more affirmative perspective, globalization has also been celebrated as a democratizing force—decentering and redistributing power rather than consolidating it, enabling new forms of connectivity within increasingly networked societies, and facilitating frictionless flows of people and goods across borders formerly closed to such traffic by cold war formations. It is also perceived as a dynamic force for change, fostering technological innovation and formal experimentation. Not surprisingly, an avant-garde culture of architecture has welcomed globalization's affinity for agile, adaptive, and pragmatic forms of practice, and architects have been responsible for emblematic projects that have helped to give it a spectacular iconography.

To conclude, then, by returning to the question of what kind of criticism is possible in an age of globalization, we may ask more specifically: how can contemporary critical discourse in architecture find a place to insert itself between Cassandra-like warnings, on the one hand, and cynicism and an uncritical celebration that provides the smooth surfaces for globalization's destructive impacts, on the other?

Mark C. Taylor

COEVOLUTIONARY DISEQUILIBRIUM

I begin with quotations from two books, one by a leading financier and the other by a Columbia University economist. In his popular book *On Globalization,* George Soros writes: "I believe that the global capitalist system in its present form is a distortion of what ought to be a global open society."[1] He proceeds to explain: "The salient feature of globalization is that it allows financial capital to move around freely."[2] Now I must confess that it's a bit hard not to be suspicious of Soros for getting religion after he made himself wealthy within the very system he now criticizes. Joseph Stiglitz begins his book *Globalization and Its Discontents* by explaining his reasons for writing the book: "While at the World Bank, I saw firsthand the devastating effect that globalization can have on developing countries, and especially the poor within those countries. I believe that globalization—the removal of barriers to free trade and the closer integration of national economies—can be a force for good and that it has the potential to enrich everyone in the world, particularly the poor."[3] Though representing two very different points of view, Soros and Stiglitz agree on the basic definition of globalization and insist on its potential for beneficial results. Moreover, they both think that many of our current problems are the result of overly zealous market fundamentalists whose policies—and here I quote Stiglitz—are "based on a simplistic model of the market, the competitive equilibrium model, in which Adam Smith's invisible hand works, and works perfectly."[4]

I want to make two points about the preoccupation with economic analysis when considering globalization. First, I would like to suggest why the models of market fundamentalists are wrong and what kind of models might be more adequate. Second, I want to insist that by interpreting globalization primarily if not exclusively in economic terms, Soros, Stiglitz, and many others take a far too limited view of this complex process.

Modern economic theory effectively begins with the application of the principle of equilibrium to economic processes. Many economists, it seems, have physics envy. While the principle of equilibrium has been used in a variety of ways over the years, in the Efficient Market Hypothesis it leads to the notion of one price. When markets are efficient—that is to say, when information is equally distributed and widely available—

there ought to be no price differential for a given commodity or security on different markets. The Efficient Market Hypothesis presupposes a model of markets as intrinsically stable systems. Such systems have the following characteristics:

1. CLOSURE: Once established, they are not open to outside influences or sources of energy or information.

2. DETERMINISM: The laws of these systems function universally and cannot be broken. Effects are proportionate to and can be accurately predicted from their causes.

3. REVERSIBILITY: The laws governing such systems apply in both temporal directions, so that time appears to be inconsequential to the systems.

4. OPERATION AT OR NEAR EQUILIBRIUM: The closure of the structures and reversibility of their governing laws incline the systems toward a state of inertia. Forces and counterforces as well as actions and reactions tend to balance each other out.

5. INDEPENDENT PARTS: In intrinsically stable systems, parts are independent of each other and thus are externally related. The whole is the sum of its parts. Since the independent parts are not fundamentally changed by their place in the whole, the whole can be reduced to the parts that comprise it.

If financial markets in the 1990s taught us anything, it is that models matter. Much of the economic theory that has come out of the University of Chicago, which has been so important for neo-liberalism over the past couple of decades, implicitly presupposes that the principles of intrinsically stable systems apply in analyzing markets. In the late 1990s, these theories and the trading models to which they gave rise brought the entire global economy perilously close to meltdown. When the map doesn't fit the territory, the consequences can be disastrous.

The shift from an industrial to an information society has resulted in a network economy with a distinctive architecture and operational logic. The network economy is an emergent complex adaptive system. In contrast to intrinsically stable systems, complex adaptive systems share the following characteristics:

1. They are comprised of many different parts, which are connected in multiple ways.

2. Diverse components interact both serially and in parallel to generate sequential as well as simultaneous effects and events.

3. Complex systems display spontaneous self-organization. Order emerges without being planned or programmed.

4. The structures emerging from spontaneous self-organization are not necessarily reducible to the aggregate of the components or elements of the systems.

5. Though generated by local interactions, emergent properties tend to be global.

6. Inasmuch as self-organizing structures emerge spontaneously, complex systems are neither fixed nor static but develop or evolve. Such evolution presupposes that complex systems are both open and adaptive. Guided by positive as well as negative feedback, development is not always incremental or continuous but can be episodic or discontinuous.

7. Emergence occurs in a narrow space lying between conditions that are too ordered and too disordered. This boundary or margin is "the edge of chaos," which is always far from equilibrium.

Two salient examples of such complex adaptive systems are the Internet and global financial markets. Inasmuch as contemporary global capital is a network effect, the logic of global capital is the logic of complex adaptive systems.

Processes of globalization, however, cannot be adequately grasped simply in economic terms. Financial markets are nodes in worldwide webs that include media, entertainment, technology, information, and even transportation networks ranging from the local to the global. Within these networks, information is not limited to what can be transmitted across cables, fiber-optic lines, and wireless devices but extends to social, economic, and even natural processes, which create and sustain life. Information, in other words, is distributed throughout social, cultural, and natural systems. This distributed information subverts the classical opposition between superstructure and infrastructure, which every form of reductive analysis presupposes. Rather than reducing cultural phenomena to economic, biological, or social explanations, nature, society, and culture are entangled in intricate feedback and feed-forward loops. In other words, nature, society, and culture are coimplicated in such a way that each is a condition of the others, and accordingly, all are mutually constitutive.

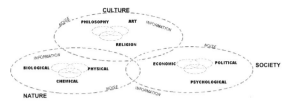

If analysis of these networks is to be persuasive, there can be no one-way streets; interpretation must always be at least two-way. But even this depiction is oversimplified. First, each of these three major loops—culture, nature, and society—is made up of other loops comprised of yet further loops. For instance, culture includes the spheres of philosophy, art, and religion; nature incorporates the physical, chemical, and biological; and society embraces economics, politics, and psychology. The structure that emerges from these tangled networks is fractal—that is, the iteration of the microstructure generates the macrostructure and the operation of the macrostructure sustains the microstructure. Accordingly, micro- and macrostructures are isomorphic. The second complication that must be added is the evolutionary component. The diagram represents a synchronic slice of a diachronic process. All of the loops and loops within loops must be set in motion. Since the structure of coimplication engenders relations of mutual constitution, nature, society, and culture are involved in a coevolutionary process. This coevolutionary process, as well as the networks through which it emerges, is a complex adaptive system.

The problem of globalization poses several issues for architecture. The networks through which distributed information circulates have an architecture whose dynamics we do not yet understand or appreciate. Much current criticism remains committed to and limited by outdated ideologies and models. To move beyond this critical impasse, it is necessary to develop a more sophisticated account of the complex coimplication and coevolution of natural, social, political, economic, and cultural processes. To meet this challenge, it will be necessary to open lines of communication between architecture and the arts, humanities, and the social and natural sciences that have been closed for far too long.

1. George Soros, *On Globalization* (New York: Public Affairs, 2002), vii.
2. Soros, *On Globalization*, 3.
3. Joseph Stiglitz, *Globalization and Its Discontents* (New York: W. W. Norton, 2002), ix.
4. Stiglitz, *Globalization and Its Discontents*, 74.

Globalization and an Architecture of Unsettlement

Saskia Sassen

What is it we're trying to name when we use the term *globalization*? Answering this question requires much decoding of messy and complex configurations. One undeniable effect of globalization is that it unsettles existing arrangements, creating rhetorical and operational openings for novel types of actors and dynamics. It makes visible social formations that are not formal and that may never become formalized.

Three main issues must be considered in the development of a critical praxis around globalization. First, how do we approach the nonformal in a world that seems to push constantly toward formalizing (most visibly exemplified in the explosion of claims for intellectual property rights)? A second issue has to do with globality and cosmopolitanism: I want to insert a variation on the theme of globality and argue that there are noncosmopolitan forms of globality. The third issue concerns the growth of digital interactive technologies, which are profoundly connected to globalization.

FORMAL AND NONFORMAL GLOBAL POLITICAL GEOGRAPHIES

Since the beginning of 2003, we have seen several political geographies emerging out of the American war on Iraq and the debates surrounding it. The first is the reinvigorated political geography of national states. These states are reinserting themselves in domains where they had been displaced partly by economic and cultural globalizations. While they comprise an older political geography conceivably drawing its last breath, they are nonetheless still powerful. A second emerging political geography is a new kind of bipolarity: not since the end of the cold war have we seen the world divided so clearly into anti- and pro-American camps. This development raises the possibility of an alternative power project to that of the United States. In terms of the global economy, there is a rift between a bloc led by the United States and another led by France, Germany, Russia, and China. These blocs are not formalized but are in development. The third political geography is shaped by the practices of informal actors rather than by states or corporations. Many activists are forming global networks that bypass the political geography of national states and international firms and markets. This signals a disposition on the part of individuals to think of themselves as part of a global project, as in Europe, where many gathered to protest the war on Iraq regardless of the position of their national leaders. Even if these individuals do not travel or cross borders, they are engaging in practices that constitute a form of globality. Citizens are going past their governments. This is a kind of political geography constituted through informal practices and is largely an ideational space.

TOWARD NONCOSMOPOLITAN FORMS OF GLOBALITY

Globalism and cosmopolitanism are often assumed to go hand in hand. But an examination of professional financial elites provides an example of how this is not the case. Although they are indeed global and may be cosmopolitan in their tastes for clothing, food, and architecture, what they do as global financial professionals is not cosmopolitan, since they are guided by a single logic: making money.

What interests me is the obverse of the typical framing of globality as cosmopolitanism, the possibility that globality includes the noncosmopolitan: elements that, unlike the WTO, IMF, and electronic markets, are not self-evidently global in scale. They occur at the local and subnational levels but emerge as forms of globality because they recur in locality after locality around the world. This is the case with many environmental struggles that are deeply localized: their participants may never travel and may be too poor to

move, but they increasingly recognize themselves as being part of global networks with ties to similarly localized efforts elsewhere. As with the financiers, these "local" globalists are noncosmopolitan in the sense that they are often obsessed with a single issue, such as the water or air quality in their village. Yet both groups are part of emergent global assemblages—the global financial market in one case and global activist networks and struggles in the other. The figurative distances traveled by this second group are longer, and their accomplishment is greater, especially considering that the actors are often poor. This example again demonstrates the multivalence of globalization: it is not simply all bad or all good.

What does the existence of forms of locally scaled globality mean for architectural practice? One possible implication is that global architecture need not transcend localized meanings or take the form of hyperarchitecture (which is often aligned with the hyperspace of global business). The forms of globality may be more diversified than those we are familiar with today.

DIGITAL FORMATIONS

Major actors in the global economy and polity have the power to advance their social logics under the guise of new technologies. Digital spaces are part of real life, no matter how "virtual": electronic markets and early warning systems stretch the world of the social into electronic space. Contrary to technological readings of the digital realm that evict social logics from consideration, electronic space is not neutral. As architects use digital tools more and more intensively, it is crucial that they recognize the social logics embedded in what might be experienced or represented as a neutral technological space.

Globalization makes possible the rise of new formations such as global finance but also the rise of new forms of empowerment among those who lack everything; it unsettles the status quo and other formalized arrangements. What kinds of practices and heuristics—both architectural and social—might allow us to seize this moment of unsettlement?

Hilary Koob-Sassen, video stills from *The Paraculture*, a work in production at the ZKM New Media Museum in Karlsruhe, Germany

Colin Fournier

"A Friendly Alien": The Graz Kunsthaus

When Sigmund Freud came to visit America, a crowd of believers greeted him as his ship docked in New York. He is reputed to have murmured to a fellow traveler: "These poor people, don't they realize that I am bringing them the plague?" In this surprisingly pessimistic and prescient statement, Freud was expressing two grave concerns: first, that the praxis, if not the fundamental theory of psychoanalysis, nurtured as it was in the penumbra of number 19 Berggasse, might not be applicable to another culture, and second, that what was being exported, indeed globalized, was a derivative product, a mere formula once severed from the critical debate that had surrounded it on its terrain of origin.

This also applies to the globalization of architecture: the products travel widely, largely indifferent to context, and the admittedly already tiny amount of genuine criticism adorning the architectural media does not follow. The result is that work can be produced abroad largely unfettered by criticism. This can be a good

or a bad thing: good buildings are built in remote parts by authors who would never have been allowed to build them back home; on the other hand, many mediocre projects go up as well, such as the derivative architecture and urbanism that Americans and Europeans are now relentlessly exporting to China.

The art museum that Peter Cook and I are currently building in Austria could certainly not have been done in London. This is no great global leap perhaps, and as an example of globalization, it is nowhere near as devastating as the spread of psychoanalysis across North America or of generic skyscrapers across China, but nevertheless it is pertinent to the issue.

Indeed the project is totally alien to its context. It is a creature from another planet and it playfully proclaims its otherness. Yet I would argue that in architecture, as in cultural evolution in general, the injection of alien elements, whether prompted from the inside by indigenous designers or by outsiders, is

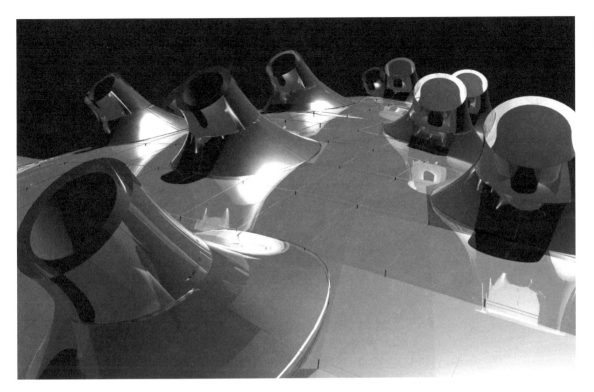

vital for the survival of cities. From this perspective and in small doses, the process of globalization, understood as the ability for cultural seeds to travel far afield and land in odd and unsuspecting places, may be found to have an acceptable face and has always had an important role as a welcome and essential catalyst of urban mutation.

The particularity of Graz as a landing place is that, unlike Vienna, the city, acting as cultural capital of Europe for 2003, has always been fairly receptive to the presence of the "other," as evidenced by the deviant and provocative projects coming out of the Grazer Schüle in the past fifty years. Volker Giencke's exotic Palm House, arguably the best and most original recent building in Graz, effectively challenges architects coming to the city to experiment even more radically.

The Kunsthaus attempts to do just that by exploiting the fact that the new museum will not house a permanent art collection. It is not intended to celebrate the memory of accumulated treasures. The contents will change constantly. The museum has, in effect, no permanent substance. Freed from the obligation to fit its form to any particular program, the building chooses to retain a mysterious presence, not only in terms of its outer manifestation (its skin is lined with an electronic layer that allows it to change its appearance) but also, and mainly, in terms of its fundamental operational concept: the internal space is a "black box" that can be modified at will by guest curators. Each visit to the museum should reveal a different configuration and offer the surprise of a new building. Not content with being an alien from the start, the museum is programmed to constantly refresh its otherness.

As far as one can tell from reactions so far, critical response to this unpredictable foreign implant, this local manifestation of the global spread of shifty non-Euclidean geometries, is positive, especially judging by the enthusiastic interest of young children, the only true aliens, and at once the most generous and toughest of critics.

From left: Interpretation by a local child of the "friendly alien"; rendering of Graz Kunsthaus, Graz, Austria, 2003

Enrique Norten

National School of Art and Design, Mexico City, 1996–2002

QUESTIONING GLOBAL ARCHITECTURE

As I was thinking about the terms *globalization* and *criticism,* I didn't find many answers, but I came up with a series of questions.

1. Why should I comment on the subject of globalization and criticism? I am an architect, not a historian or a critic. I decided to be an architect because I love to build. And I build wherever institutions or individuals appreciate what I do, which happens to be in many places. Does that make me a global architect?

2. We are all part of a global network, a complex inter-connectivity where ideas, images, and products flow freely throughout the world. Most architects practicing today use a common vocabulary inherited from modernity that allows us to share images and ideas in a universal manner. Does that make us global architects?

3. Architecture is a site-specific activity. Building is about the particularities and the uniqueness of the places where we have the opportunity to build. Every site is made of a superimposition of many layers of information. The opacities and transparencies created by this superimposition of layers produce the uniqueness of the place. Is the collection of unique places like a fractal, a combination of small patterns into the larger patterns of contemporary architecture?

4. Although New York is one center for architectural criticism, today we are living in a condition of polycentrism. Each global center generates a set of parameters and conditions that overlap to create undefined zones that are interesting for both architecture and architectural criticism. Are those peripheries part of the global discourse?

5. Globalization is an overused word with many different meanings. When we speak as architects or as architecture critics about a global condition or about globalization, to what are we really referring?

6. When we discuss global architecture, what aspect of architecture do we mean? Do we mean architecture as a form of art, as a discipline, or as a practice? It is very difficult to try to define architecture in these times. I've always held that although architecture is a form of art, architects are not artists.

7. As architects, when we make architecture, are we at the same time engaging in a form of critical discourse? Is architecture itself a kind of criticism? If so, what is the criticism about? Is it about institutions, world systems, or architecture itself? Does a critical practice of architecture exist?

8. How are contemporary practices of architecture different from the dogmatic practices of our predecessors, the first generation of modern architects, who proposed a global condition of architecture that they called the International style? I believe that our practice is more global, not because we are melting into an amorphous world culture but because the architects of my generation are able to understand the uniqueness of multiple places. Because we have the opportunity to discuss and practice architecture in these particular sites, we are becoming more local, individual, differentiated, and paradoxically, more global.

Terence Riley

The Global and the Local

Recently, *globalization* has come to eclipse the usage of designations such as "international," "transnational," or "multinational," without much consideration for the differences in meaning between them. I would argue that *globalism* represents a concept quite different from the interrelated meanings of inter-, trans-, and multinationalism. The latter are all based on the notion of nation-states and national identity as a first condition, which gives rise to a new phenomenon when some national characteristic or product crosses political and cultural boundaries without losing its origin. The phenomenon may appear globally, but where it comes from remains key in understanding it.

The term *globalism* has acquired a different meaning in that it has come to represent phenomena that might appear anywhere and everywhere. Furthermore, the origins of these phenomena may not only be obscure but also irrelevant. The Internet is a prime example of this. The question "Where does the Internet come from?" does not have an answer that provides any

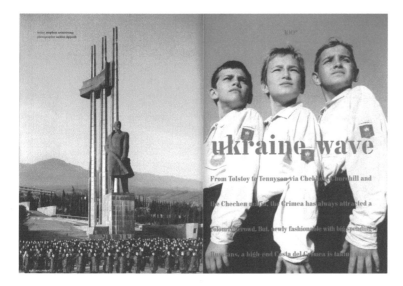

writer stephen armstrong
photographer achim lippoth

ukraine wave

From Tolstoy to Tennyson via Chekhov, Churchill and the Chechen mafia, the Crimea has always attracted a colourful crowd. But, newly fashionable with big spending Russians, a high-end Costa del Crimea is taking shape

deeper understanding of its structure and function.

Given these distinctions, can we really say that architecture, something that is so rooted in its place, can be global? A good argument might be made that the technical and commercial language of high-rise real estate development has become so perfected worldwide that the specific historical origins of the skyscraper in late-nineteenth-century Chicago are no longer relevant. But can an architect really practice globally, that is, beyond national identity? Despite all the rhetoric, aren't such global figures as Rem Koolhaas, Norman Foster, and Frank Gehry, as well as corporations like SOM, defined to a large extent—by themselves and others—in terms of nationality? They may seem to be everywhere, but to understand them and their work it remains very important to know where they are from. Whether or not architecture is able to become truly a global phenomenon, it is interesting to note that it has not shown up on the radar of antiglobalization protesters, as far as I know. While much has been made of defending local cultures, agriculture, cuisine, languages, and environments, the threat—if not reality—of global architecture

curiously does not seem to raise the same anxieties.

Regarding criticism, we might ask if it can be global and maintain a critical effect. It can be argued that the less critical the media is, the more global its reach and the greater its influence. Magazines such as *Wallpaper* are referred to as glossies because of the type of paper they are printed on. Equally glossy, however, are their editorial positions, which tend to avoid the issues that create critical friction. Recalling the expression "All politics is local," it might also be argued that criticality can only operate on a localized, if not local, basis. It seems that it is only in these situations that the critical dialogue between artist and audience can develop and cohere.

From left: Demonstration by Action Group for Better Architecture in New York, in front of Penn Station, August 2, 1963; spread from *Wallpaper* magazine

SPEAKING OF GLOBALIZATION AND CRITICISM

Gwendolyn Wright

I would like to reflect for a moment on language by decoding some of the key words frequently used in recent architectural events and publications that take up the topic of globalization. Language provides delight, of course: familiar incantations may renew one's beliefs; distinctive phrases may capture new insights with their freshness. But words, like images, quickly become clichés, losing their original capacity to make someone listen and think. Language provides a powerful means for clarification, communication, and inquiry, but also for obfuscation and self-deception; to use it effectively requires self-conscious exploration and precision, as well as play and surprise.

Let's start with the word *globalization.* The various cognates of the term build on previous "internationalist" views of the world without shedding internationalism's self-centered parochialism and idealized vision of a commonality that radiates from the center outward. To be sure, there are unprecedented social and economic opportunities in our "global" realm, as well as high-speed linkages that facilitate contact. Yet architects must also take note of the loss, deprivation, isolation, and increased inequalities that characterize globalization, both in the world at large and in every particular city, each one part of a worldwide pattern and yet distinct in its own form. It is always worth asking: how might we, as architects, smooth blockages and address inequalities in the so-called global flow? We should experiment more fully with the idea that architecture has multiple effects, intended and unexpected, global and local.

What then do we mean by the "local"? Many architects assume that the local is inexorably provincial, backward, or nostalgic. For others, especially neotraditionalists, the local seems inherently benign and inclusive. Why not reconfigure the word as a term of cultural specificity and creative engagement? Every building is inevitably related to its particular locale in multiple ways, affecting the surrounding streets, social life, and future development. However, "local" also refers to a variety of close relationships, including those not necessarily grounded in physical proximity. In this sense, architecture culture itself is a non-place-based local community, one that relies on internal cohesion and diversity, responds to the conditions of a surrounding culture, and connects with other systems, both near and far.

If we acknowledge the ambiguities in architectural rhetoric, the answer certainly isn't fashionable new terms or neologisms. Architects must instead ask how our language—verbal and visual, collective and personal—represents and challenges our values, affects actual practices, and obscures inactions or inattention. This is not to say that words always determine meaning, nor that architects inevitably do what they say or write. But it's far too easy simply to attack those who don't understand, or to assert the babble of "archi-talk" as a right (or a sign) of the avant-garde. There is no formula or code for what languages mean, what they do, and to whom they speak. There is, however, both a responsibility and a joy in asking questions, over and over again, about even the smallest elements of architectural discourse.

THE LANGUAGE OF GLOBAL ARCHITECTURE

Yehuda Safran

Thinking about the state of architecture at the beginning of the twenty-first century, I'm reminded of Italo Calvino's "Six Memos for the Next Millennium," which he did not live to deliver; in fact, he did not even live to write the sixth one, which was simply entitled "Consistency." Indeed, I wonder whether this last memo could really have been written, since what we experience today above all is a sense of inconsistency. I think that the key to how architecture will develop is precisely how we as architects and architecture critics use language. Or the way that language uses us.

Words often precede acts of building, but words themselves are also a form of acting or making. For instance, Peter Cook, who is currently collaborating with Colin Fournier on a remarkable museum in Graz, Austria, spent many years incubating his ideas in London. The city is an ideal place for trying out concepts in the form of words and testing words as actions.

Last fall, I went to the Shanghai Biennial, an event that is undeniably a product of globalization. After the Biennial, I flew to Chengdu, the capital of Sichuan province, where I met an architect named Liu Jiakun. There, in the middle of China, he showed me his work, which immediately made me think of works by Carlo Scarpa, Alvaro Siza, and Luis Barragán. As it turned out, Liu Jiakun did not speak any other language than Chinese. And yet he was working fluently within the critical discourse of modernism. The example of Liu Jiakun demonstrates that to be critical, a work need not be regionalist, and insofar as it is only regional in scope, its critical effect may be circumscribed.

While I believe that where we come from is important, beyond a certain point origin no longer matters. Place, on the other hand, does. Zaha Hadid, for instance, could not have developed the work she has done if she had stayed in Baghdad. We gravitate toward those places—or people—where and in whom we can hope for some understanding of what we are saying. In other words, a language community—even one that spans different vernaculars—is the sine qua non of any future architecture.

The term *architect* encompasses far more than "one engaged in the art of building." Today, an architect is one who manages information, designs web sites, and decides foreign policy—in short, someone who organizes things, and does so within an ever more complex and interconnected global field.

This broadening of the term *architect* parallels a trend within architecture itself—the growing interest, at the end of the twentieth century and the beginning of the twenty-first, not just in buildings but also in what happens inside them: programs, events, and the movement of bodies. Architects have become not only designers of the stage set but also choreographers of human activities. While this has generated exciting possibilities for rethinking architectural practice, it has also raised new questions. What is the nature of the human subject that architecture organizes—docile or free, natured or nurtured? Can architecture in turn shape or produce the subject?

Reinhold Martin and Sanford Kwinter are concerned less with the subjects shaped by architecture than with how architects themselves are influenced by contemporary global conditions, including the lauded network economy—what Martin calls the "organizational complex." He prescribes a few points to help architects negotiate contemporary fields of power, beginning with the slogan "Think different." Kwinter offers some prescriptions and predictions of his own for how architects might seize upon their current position at the "probe head of culture." As architecture is absorbed into the knowledge industry, and the role of the architect shifts from building to organizing social relations, architects, he suggests, should rethink their approaches to the digital realm and to older formations like the city.

On the subject that inhabits architecture, Elizabeth Grosz provides a philosophical meditation on the nature of the body and its use of prostheses to extend its capacities and desires. Can architecture, she asks, be thought of as a prosthetic device? Christian Girard is also interested in the prosthetic. Through a series of photographs, he traces the history of technology's influence on the body, a body rendered increasingly docile through its inscription by the market.

Catherine Ingraham notes that the relationship between architecture and its inhabitants, between the inanimate and the animate, is marked by a historical asymmetry and wonders how contemporary architectural practices might unsettle this hierarchy. Lars Spuybroek draws on the lessons provided by a classic psychological experiment to understand how the eye and body operate in tandem to perceive space. He argues that perception and movement are linked by tectonics, the art of architectural construction. And Ed Keller addresses the freedom of the body, calling attention to the importance of time as a medium of control. Architects, he asserts, can identify systems of temporal control and help to liberate the body.

Reinhold Martin

FROM THE OEDIPUS COMPLEX TO THE ORGANIZATIONAL COMPLEX

At the start of the twentieth century, the kind of institutional power typically passing through architecture's channels, from courthouses to private homes, was for the most part still organized according to top-down, patriarchal diagrams like family trees. In that sense, if we take organization to mean the production and management of bodies in space and time, including their forms, movements, desires, and dreams, the bodies produced by these hierarchies—including both people and buildings—were bound by the imperatives of the Oedipus complex, a decidedly phallogocentric affair in which the child usurped the position of the father while leaving the tree itself intact. Another name for this, it could be said, was "evolution."

The dawn of the digital age in the mid-twentieth century saw a gradual rearrangement of such diagrams, whereby power increasingly abandoned the old form of the father sitting atop the tree and was redistributed into low-lying horizontal networks organized dynamically around multiple feedback loops and decentralized, redundant nodes. These were open systems, premised on the notions of self-organization and emergence. Another name for this, by the 1990s, was the "new economy." As manifest in architecture, we might call this new diagram the "organizational complex."

If one allows for the possibility of such a displacement, some of the challenges facing architecture today come into sharper focus. For example, in a profession

controlled by faceless networks with mysterious acronyms like SOM, the cult of personality and the mass production of signatures may only be further evidence that the heroic

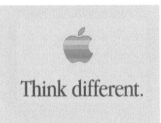

public image of the "architect" is essentially a media effect, a phantasm. But does this reduce architects and their buildings to mere empty shells floating across a vast corporate sea of capital, goods, and services? Not necessarily. Organization is not just a map with dots and arrows; it is also an image—a logo, sound bite, brand, or flag—and none of these are in short architectural supply. The new corporations enforce disciplinary as well as spatiotemporal organization, mandating—at the level of both logistics and "Imagineering"—unity, cohesion, and brand loyalty, to say nothing of the repressive togetherness of a nation at war.

So what is to be done? Well, first, "Think different," as they used to say at Apple Computer. But beware: the dynamic assimilation and incorporation of difference itself, in place of resemblance, filiation, and the old family trees, is—for better or worse—a hallmark of the new networks of power. Michael Hardt and Antonio Negri said it best in defining the new global regime they call "Empire," to which the organizational complex belongs: "Empire manages hybrid identities, flexible hierarchies, and plural exchanges through modulating networks of command. The distinct national colors of the [old] imperialist map of the world have merged and blended in the [new] imperial global rainbow."[1]

Under these new conditions, a kinder, gentler, more flexible and dynamic form of organization, incubated in the multinational corporations, operates at the cutting edge of corporate globalization. In obediently advocating a go-with-the-flow, "I'm-just-an-architect" alliance with the forces now reorganizing the oil fields in Iraq, recent architectural discourse and practice have risked the possibility that all architecture today is, in effect, corporate architecture.

So again, what is to be done? Well, here are a few tips—a kind of group therapy for the discipline—on how to deal with the organizational complex.

1. MAKE IT VISIBLE. Like the military-entertainment complex that underlies it, the organizational complex depends both on stealth and on the blinding glare of spectacle, celebrity, and symbolism. So learn to recognize it when you see it.

2. DO NOT EMULATE IT. There is no body more docile than a self-organizing system, biological or otherwise—not only because its instabilities ultimately serve the stability of the "system" as such but because they secretly maintain the longed-for stability of a well-organized, well-disciplined "self."

3. INFILTRATE IT. Work from within—but not like a sycophantic "embedded reporter" identified with the war machine. Rather, aspire to the unverifiable autonomy of the double agent. It should never be entirely clear which side you're on.

4. COUNTER-ORGANIZE. Don't rely on cookbook design processes and pseudo-digital diagrams to produce architecture for you. Use your imagination, strategically. And never naturalize.

5. EXCEED ITS TOLERANCES. The one thing the organizational complex cannot tolerate is utopia, which died along with Oedipus. A new architecture, secretly being prepared in hidden laboratories and think tanks, will conjure utopia's ghost in a thousand different forms through counterintelligence and cunning. Call this new architecture a "visionary realism."

And finally: "Have a nice day."

1. Michael Hardt and Antonio Negri, *Empire* (Cambridge, Mass.: Harvard University Press, 2000), xii–xiii.

Four Arguments for the Elimination of Architecture (Long Live Architecture)

Sanford Kwinter

The present appears to be a golden moment for architecture: public awareness and general lust for design are at an all-time high; everyone is clearly doing brilliant and fresh work; architects are becoming increasingly respected and sought out for their ideas about social developments, history, and the city; and it seems that we have all gotten over our objections to capitalism. Despite some of these ironies, such developments in themselves are not a bad thing.

But isn't something being masked by all the happiness? Is this the classic "manic defense"? Not to get all heavy now, but perhaps what we're hiding from ourselves is the fear of the second act. Architecture's only partly willing catapult to the probe head of culture in the last five years has brought responsibilities that architects do not seem altogether ready to face. What are some of these challenging realities? Frankly, I can't know, so I have made up a few just to see how it makes us feel, and perhaps to prepare us to face our inflexibilities, sacred cows, and the limits of our courage, ambition, and imaginations.

First, we need to face the fact that architecture is fast becoming part of the knowledge industry. "Design" is becoming increasingly dissociated from simple "building" and increasingly associated with the production of intellectual property: ideas, routines, contexts, entire social and cultural environments. Every social relation is now a target of design, not only relations of humans to objects and humans to concrete environments but of humans to humans and humans to collective and symbolic enterprises as well. Architects now are inventors of those intervening "films" that seem to coat everything these days and that one used to call "interfaces." Now more than ever, the reshaping of the knowledge system is inseparable from the transformation of the material environment.

Architects must adapt to this emerging reality.

Second, we must acknowledge that there may not even be architects in thirty years. Why? Because the material of the world is generated largely through administrative apparatuses (or what is more benignly referred to as "organization"). A few architects long ago anticipated the shift of their role from building, traditionally conceived, to being organizers of social relations. Some seized upon program as the new motor of social invention and production. It may take some time before the transformation is complete, but at that time the architects who still design buildings and other details will be employed by "program designers," just as draftspersons are now employed to render what architects have dreamed up.

Third, the age of the computer and the euphoria for all things "virtual" may already be over. Architecture may well have overinvested in an arguably necessary fad. No one who has called the computer a "tool" has ever betrayed the slightest idea of what a computer is. And I don't mean to argue that they are simply shortsighted rubes largely unaware of the broader environmental implications and impacts of informational and corporal automation as it is taking place at the current scale (though they are at least partly this). I mean that those who consider the computer a tool appear to have no inkling of what a truly marvelous concoction a computer really represents, because they obediently and conventionally conceive of it as "digital" when in fact it is quite demonstrably an analog organization (made of glass, silicon, and electricity). By extension, and more important, there appears to be nothing in the software universe that is not derived from the analysis of real-world material processes. Nurb splines, for example, bend like wood slats even though they don't have to.

Student research in Toshiko Mori's seminar at Harvard in 2001 has demonstrated convincingly that today's most successful digital design algorithms are actually based on weaving matrixes largely derived from, abstracted from, or modeled after real material continuums. Computers are not so much tools as hyperbolic versions of real continuums. They allow us to capture the movement of matter and to manipulate and redeploy physical traits, qualities, and behaviors into novel composites. The future lies in getting our heads back on straight. We should redirect research from the screen-based simulations that predominated in the last fifteen years toward the considerably greater intelligence that is already impressed into matter, including investigation of new scientific and industrial processes and the new materials in which these processes are embedded.

Fourth, although the city has disappeared, it is nevertheless here to stay—a clumsy paradox. We no longer know where to look to find the glorious ensembles and performances that we once called the "city." In a modern economy, the city is not just where we are, it is who we are, and the parochialism that has been so enjoyable and fruitful in these last few decades may already have come to an end. The first sign was the shibboleth "globalization," another was "markets," and today it could well be the twin concepts of "jihad" and "war on . . ." Either way, these are all concepts that effectively join every human on the planet into a direct and ruthless symbiotic relationship where the credit of one entails the deficit of the other. This implies a new spatial condition, and however difficult it may be, it is the new "city" we live in. Design will see its safe havens of traditional, poetic, and academic form-making shrunk, trimmed, and challenged by these new social and historical demands.

The present is undeniably a period of radical transition. Architecture must undergo an explosive and disfiguring transformation that will either carry it toward a necessary if slightly cold cosmopolitanism; otherwise, it can retreat to face the prospects of mediocrity, provincialism, even irrelevance. What is certain is that in coming of age we have lost the option of standing still.

Elizabeth Grosz

PROSTHETIC OBJECTS

The body has a capacity for prosthetic extension, a capacity to link to objects in ways never conceived before, to incorporate objects into its daily operations, to become social and historical in the most fundamental sense. A living body is a duality—not of mind and body but rather of an inside and an outside, two overlapping and superimposable ever-changing networks, separated by a relatively porous sac, an epidermal clothing or biological architecture, yet linked through ingestion and practice. How we understand the status and ontological implication of prostheses dictates how we understand the relations between this inside and the outside.

What is the nature of this inside with its own passions and actions, its own orientations and drives, that requires an outside to give it its internal structuring? And what is this outside, an outside of events, acts, and processes, both benign and catastrophic, that affects, transforms, structures, and completes the inside? More concretely and architecturally, what must a body, a "subject," be to invariably make, inhabit, and transform architecture? What is architecture such that it excites and transforms the body or bodies that inhabit it?

Human, animal, and insect bodies are prosthetic; they acquire and utilize supplementary objects through an incorporation that enables the objects to function as if they were bodily organs: creatures use tools, ornaments, and appliances to augment their bodily capacities. Are their bodies lacking something, which they need to replace with artificial or substitute organs? Should prostheses be conceived, according to a model of practical reason, as substitute organs, organs that duplicate or approximate and replace missing or impaired limbs and organs and enable the body to function according to its preestablished pattern of performance (as in artificial legs, glasses, and contact lenses)? In this model, prostheses are organized by utility: the body and its functions are understood in terms of pregiven possibilities of movement and action, and prostheses restore these functions to the newly reconstituted yet partly artificial organic totality.

Or conversely, should prostheses be understood, in terms of aesthetic reorganization and proliferation, as the consequence of an inventiveness that functions beyond and perhaps in defiance of pragmatic need? Are prosthetic bodies excessive, capable of more activities than their given limbs and organs allow? Here prostheses must be regarded not as a confirmation of pregiven actions but as an opening up of actions that may not have been possible before. Prostheses actualize virtualities that the natural body cannot realize, inducing a mutual metamorphosis, transforming both the body supplemented and the object that supplements it. One might ask more specifically: is architecture a natural extension of the living body through an accommodation of external objects? Or is architecture a denaturalization, an enculturation, part of an endless and ongoing socialization and thus a transformation of human form?

Sigmund Freud understood man's relation to objects as one of extension: through the acquisition of clothing, armor, and housing, man extends his relatively fragile and precarious reach over the world of objects, amplifying his bodily capacities and extending and cathecting the ego's libidinal reach; in making himself more than himself, man becomes master of more than he can directly touch. In his fantasy of omnipotence, man approaches the status of "prosthetic god":

> With every tool [man] is perfecting his own organs, whether motor or sensory, or is removing the limits to their functioning. Motor power places gigantic forces at his disposal, which, like his muscles, he can employ in any direction; thanks to ship and aircraft neither water nor air can hinder his movements . . . Man has, as it were, become a kind of prosthetic God. When he puts on all his auxiliary organs he is truly magnificent, but these organs have not grown onto him and they still give him much trouble at times.[1]

Instruments enable man to become more than he is, to attain a future in which his bodily form poses no obstacle to his aspirations: man transforms the world according to his interests and in the process he transforms himself in ways that he does not understand or control. The objects that enrich him through the harnessing of their material resources become his property or territory, his colonies, even though he is no longer at home in this world that he now surveys with magisterial authority.

Henri Bergson too affirms the fundamentally prosthetic nature of intelligence in its close and continuing tie with material invention, with the unexpected use of what is found. Invention accelerates the rate of change beyond its biological speed—tools, for example, invented and used for specific purposes, are incorporated and transformed at a much greater rate than evolutionary change itself. This change in material environment is precisely the invention and intervention of the customary, the social, and the historical into the biological, for which the biological prepares itself through the elaboration and development of intelligence: "All the elementary forces of the intellect tend to transform matter into an instrument of action, that is, in the etymological sense of the word, into an *organ* . . . inorganic matter itself, converted into an immense organ by the industry of the living being."[2]

For Freud, man expands himself—his narcissistic reach over the world—by incorporating external objects. These external objects are rendered objects for man, but they become reduced in the process: they are no longer wood, plastic, or minerals but a leg, an arm, spectacles. For Bergson, life expands itself by generating new capacities in both the living being and in the prosthetic object. The object is always, for him, reduced by its perception by and usefulness to an observer: its multiple facets are simplified and narrowed to those qualities that life can extract from it. But equally, objects, in being extricated from the multiplicity of connections they exert in the material world, are given new qualities, new capacities, a virtuality that they lack in nature. Intelligence endows objects with virtuality while "stealing" from them all the qualities that are considered useful or relevant. The living being and the objects, now rendered prosthetic, transform each other, undergoing a not entirely determinable "becoming" through their interaction. The living transforms non-living objects, and these objects, in turn, transform the parameters and possibilities of life.

Can other living beings, cultural institutions, and social practices be construed as prosthetic? Is a virus prosthetic to its host, are slave ants prostheses for their ant masters, is language a human prosthesis? More pertinently, is architecture prosthetic? Does architecture complete the beings who inhabit it, much as the ant colony or bees' nest completes and overrides the needs of its inhabitants? These questions demonstrate that the division between an inside and an outside, an object and a prosthesis, a natural organ and an artificial organ, a body and what augments it, is not clear-cut.

Is architecture the practical completion of humans' need for shelter, for social alignments and other social and biological needs? Or is architecture one of the elements directing man's "becoming" other than what he is? Undeniably, there are two—at least two—kinds of architecture, just as there are two types of prosthesis: one that accommodates existing needs, that fits into the body's current and recognized needs; and another that introduces new aesthetic possibilities not yet available, awaiting prosthetic incorporation.

1. Sigmund Freud, "Civilization and Its Discontents" (1929), in *The Standard Edition of the Complete Psychological Works of Sigmund Freud*, ed. James Strachey, vol. 19, *1923–1925: The Ego and the Id and Other Works* (London: Hogarth Press, 1995), 90–92.
2. Henri Bergson, *Creative Evolution* (1911; New York: Modern Library, 1944), 178.

Christian Girard

Back from Fast Forward: Architecture, Bodies, and Icarian Technologies

How can we combine the concepts of the event and the machine, the notion of what takes place (the event) and what is repetition (the machine)?[1] The machine and the human body have always been connected through the event, and the nature of this connection has attained a new degree of sophistication and complexity as bodies are increasingly reshaped by technology. In the past, the machine was utilized to produce movement in space, either through its own movement or through its capacity to transport bodies. However, this movement of technology often brought accidents—for example, the disaster that occurred in 1895 when a train crashed through the Montparnasse railway station. The train's midair pause is an apt example of what I call an "Icarian technology." Icarian technologies are also to be found in the arts, with the flying body of Yves

Klein in 1960; in architecture, with the *Advertisement for Architecture* (1976) by Bernard Tschumi, in which a man is caught midflight between the private space of a building and the public space of the street; and in advertising, with a billboard for vodka that presents a life-size mockup of an apartment turned on its side— essentially in flight. In all of these configurations we find architecture and bodies, including technological bodies like the steam locomotive, in awkward topological situations; they are in the suspended positions that the modern movement sought literally to build.

On the bank of the Seine in Paris, directly in front of the school where I teach, I found a vendor selling three different images of suspended bodies and events. The juxtaposition of the three images offers a reading of the city as built and lived in three modes: first, a catastrophic mode of dramatic and violent events, as embodied in the train in the sky; second, a construction/destruction/ deconstruction mode, illustrated by the half-built Eiffel Tower; and third, an intersubjective mode, represented by a famous photograph taken by Robert Doisneau of a couple kissing. In this last image, two bodies are suspended in action while other human and mechanical bodies move in the background. Doisneau used the technology of photography to produce a romantic fiction in the public space of the street. The image is staged, aptly demonstrating that even the most intersubjective and

"human" interactions can be technological effects. More and more, instead of moving bodies mechanically, technology is embedded in the body itself, and even helps produce the body.

Today in Paris at the precise location of the Montparnasse train accident stands a giant video screen billboard where one can see a couple— another image of romance and bodies—suspended in the public space above the street level. Current advertisements may be the best example of combining the event and the machine. Through technology, they seek to transform behaviors and integrate human subjects into the capitalist realm. In a recent theater poster, a human body marked with a bar code lies among the goods available for purchase at a supermarket. Bodies are increasingly for sale— bodies to be marketed, if not literally in a market. We have arrived at a point where humans are "reformatted" to become more and more predictable—artificial intelligences—with proportionately more docile bodies. Technology is encroaching not only on humans' bodies but also on our souls, folding everything into the abstract realm of capital.

1. Jacques Derrida, "Le ruban de machine à écrire? Limited Ink III," in *Papier Machine* (Paris: Editions Galilée, 2001), 37 (author's translation). The original text reads: "Pourrons-nous un jour, et d'un seul mouvement, ajointer une pensée de l'événement avec la pensée de la machine? Pourrons-nous penser, ce qui s'appelle penser, d'un seul et d'un même coup et ce qui arrive (on nomme cela un événement), et, d'autre part, la programmation calculable d'une répétition automatique (on nomme cela une machine)?"

From left: Yves Klein, *Leap into the Void*, 1960; three modes of understanding the city; Bernard Tschumi, *Advertisements for Architecture*, 1976–77

ARCHITECTURE: THE ART OF INDIFFERENCE

Catherine Ingraham

The very idea that space is constructed as an entity independent from the bodies in it—planets, stars, human bodies—seems absurd at some level. But of course, that is the very definition of modern mathematical space. Architecture—by means of program, details, symbols—tries to direct the emptying and filling of space but is generally indifferent to who or what specifically occupies that space. It would seem too intimate a task for architecture to bring living occupants to mind in the hyperspecific way that occupants bring themselves to mind.

The "life" that uses and occupies architectural space, and from which architecture is said to derive its significance and material reality at any given moment, is the opposite of indifferent. Human life privileges itself merely by the fact of being alive—a tautology that is also an expression of the difficulty of standing back and looking at our biological hegemony. Georges Canguilhem puts it as follows: "To live is to attach value to life's purposes and experiences"; an overestimation of the value of life is a constituent part of living. Historically, in philosophy (even in Descartes) and the natural sciences, the animate is usually given the superior position with respect to the inanimate, although the categorical split between the animate and inanimate is a fairly recent development in history.

Something quite interesting results in architecture from this split between self-privileging animate bodies and indifferent, inanimate space: an asymmetry. This is not an ethical asymmetry first and foremost (I am not speaking of the sanctity of life over matter) but, instead, an asymmetry produced by the containment of movement (the plasticity of the animate) by what is not moving, or by what is moving slower. As Canguilhem also notes—referring to the brain and mind—the container and the contained cannot, by definition, speak to each other. The brain is animate but moves at a different speed, and in a different register, than the mind. Architecture is not animate, at least not in the usual sense of that word.

Life actively maintains itself by using, opportunistically, whatever is around it to survive. Architecture—like other milieux that "contain" life—is at the service of life, although this concept of service has changed drastically since antiquity. In almost every epoch, architecture has attempted to offset the inherent asymmetry of the relationship of life to space by supplying the appearance of symmetry. The history of architecture has been tightly governed by the tension and play between architecture's grounded symmetries and the human body's complex, moving equipoise. Architecture has been shaped as the discipline of a solicitous but indifferent symmetrical and grounded space on and in which narcissistic, resourceful, moving beings live.

How, in architecture, would that tension be identified? Would it be at the level of detail, ornament, or structure, or in architectural discourse and historical claims? There is clearly an ambivalence guarding the gates of the problem. Rem Koolhaas, following Le Corbusier, has experimented with actual moving parts (a moving floor for a handicapped, slower-moving occupant) and with surrogate movements (screens showing moving pictures off to the side of the building, ramps that suggest dynamism). Greg Lynn has suggested that architectural structure itself can now be made more fluid, more adaptive.

For centuries, human biological life has been without the spatial pressure exerted by geology and natural environments that contributed to its early evolution. But human life also has been defined partly by its early ability to orchestrate, through technology, its own biological niche. As a species we have long been designing spaces before moving into them. Architecture, for its part, has often looked to models of biological life and natural history for clues to its own structure and organization. But now the human life to which architecture looks—life that is in the process of transformation because of genetic research—may be losing some of its biological status. We find that we differ less than we thought we did from very simple organisms. Crossovers will occur. Space-time maps with complex, developmental surfaces have already allowed architecture to jettison its superficial symmetry (and putative verticality, a related discussion), although not yet its ground. With the computer, architecture has acquired speed and equipoise, but it still moves slower than a toddler in space. Are these baby steps toward a different kind of asymmetry?

TEXTILE TECTONICS

In 1963, Richard Held and Alan Hein conducted a classic and rather merciless neurological experiment in which two kittens were raised from birth in a carousel. One kitten was able to move freely around a circular track, while the other was strapped in a suspended gondola, which was pulled by the free cat. As the young animals' brain tissues developed, their actions and perceptions were integrated into a coherent neurological system. The free cat was able to link the act of walking to its own perceptions, while for the other, action and vision were separated. After a number of weeks, the kittens were released from the carousel. The free cat moved and behaved normally, while the other stumbled, bumped into objects, and was afflicted with agnosia—a condition of mental blindness brought on by neurological rather than physiological causes. The second cat could not coordinate its movements with what it saw because in its experience, action and perception had never existed in the same continuum. The experiment by Held and Hein proved that these two faculties were inseparable—perception relied on action and action was only possible through perception.

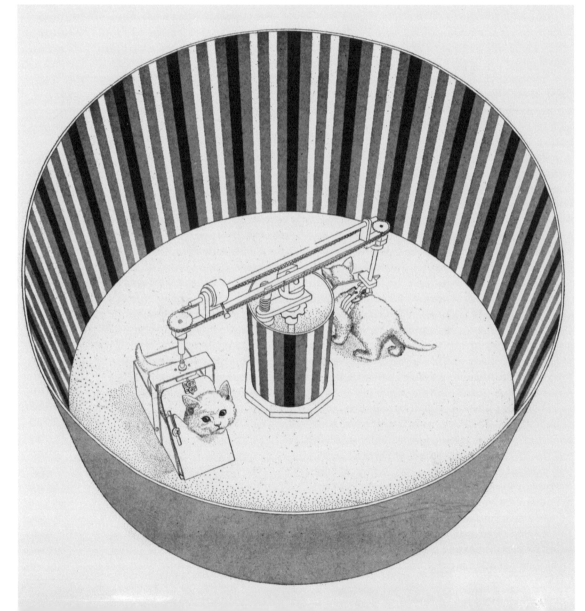

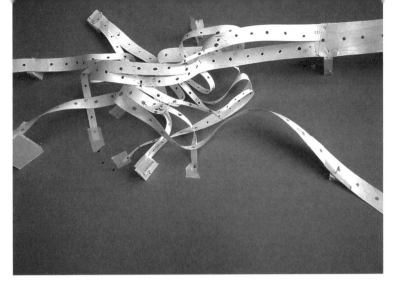

This implies something quite fundamental for architecture, where the plan is typically thought of as the surface of action and the wall as the surface of perception. Drawing from Held and Hein's experiment, architects cannot simply start with a plan and extrude it upward according to the vector of gravity to create a building or a space. Rather than accept this a priori distinction between floor and wall, action and perception, we must address the neurological continuum between these faculties and find the vector that connects them. I would argue that this link between action and perception, movement and image, is the act of construction; it is the vector of tectonics. The idea of vision as something in progress can be connected to the notion of architecture as a vector between the making and the made. Two specific projects address this relationship between action and perception, and between the making and the made, through different tectonic strategies.

Currently, we are converting an old textile factory in the center of the city of Lille, France, into an arts complex that includes a school, exhibition spaces, artists' housing, a library, and even a Turkish bath. Next to this, we are building a concert hall with rehearsal studios and offices. The project, called the Maison Folie (2000–2003), reverses the distinction, coined by Gottfried Semper, between that which carries (structure, made of hard materials like wood) and that which is carried (soft, woven materials that provide infill between structure). In contrast to the Semperian model, in which the tectonic is assumed to be located at the corners of the building, in the concert hall of the Maison Folie, the edge is spread out and woven into a surface across the facade. The geometry of the building is modulated by movement and light: the surface transforms with the sun's varying positions, changing from reflective to transparent. One's experience of the building is contingent on where one stands and at what time of day.

Another project we are building, the Son-O-House (2000–2003), in the Netherlands, also illustrates the process of action becoming structure. We began by tracing the movements of people in their houses—habituated movements, practices, actions, and scripts. These were subdivided into three interrelated scales: movements of the limbs, joints, and extremities. We then coded these three types of movements onto a strip of paper: for instance, when a hip movement (which always entails the movement of the whole body) was accompanied by a joint movement (like the flexion of an elbow or knee), the strip of paper was cut down the middle. Additional foot or hand movements were mapped by another cut. Each cut gave the paper a potential to bend sideways. We developed three such strips, each with its own pattern of cuts related to different choreographies or scripts. When we stapled these three strips together at the points where they were cut, we ended up with a complex arabesque structure.

Here we get at the core of what I call soft constructivism. The interlaced arabesque of paper is not the a priori goal of design but the complex result of an analog computing process. Instead of following the planar extrusion method, we employ a process in which the elevation feeds information back to the plan and vice versa. On its own, the strip of paper is a soft element that could not stand up, but in cooperation with others it gains a structural rigidity. In Semperian terms, it is a textile element that becomes tectonic. The relationship between rigid and soft and the hierarchy between the carrier and carried are inverted.

In connecting this self-engineered diagram to the ground surface, one obtains an interlacing effect of continuities that curl away from one another, in an operation similar to the combing of hair. By reorganizing the sweeps or curls into groups oriented according to their original direction, one starts with continuity but ends up with a system of segmentations and an object that might be described as post-blob. Instead of beginning with a standing object and then deforming it, here curvature is the intrinsic and emergent property that generates the architecture.

From left: Held and Hein's experiment on the relationship between action and perception, 1963; study model for Son-O-House, Son en Breugel, the Netherlands, 2000–2003

BODIES IN TIME

Ed Keller

Freedom and confinement are typically thought of in spatial terms—as functions of access, restriction, and movement, for instance. I would like to suggest, however, that freedom also has a temporal dimension. In the contemporary world, mechanisms of temporal control often masquerade as forms of spatial control. We are imprisoned as much by the time clock as we are by the factory or office walls, as much by our own wristwatches as we are by our physical surroundings. Henri Bergson wrote, "Wherever anything lives, there is, open somewhere, a register in which time is being inscribed."[1] In our quest for greater freedom, then, we must trace these invisible registers and track the way that time inflects bodies at scales large and small.

Architecture, though typically considered a static art, can play a role in facilitating awareness of time and, hence, freedom. As architects, we can identify mechanisms of temporal control and open them to manipulation. We must ask ourselves what kinds of time and what forms of freedom we can introduce into the world to encourage the transformation of docile bodies into subjects with a full range of intelligence and expression.

These are some of the questions that my firm, Atelier Chronotype, addresses in our recent project, *Ornament and Crime,* a work of "hard" science fiction set twenty-two years in the future. We are developing the project simultaneously as an online computer game, graphic novel, short digital animations, and two feature-length film projects. In a sense, devising a computer game is similar to creating a building: the architect designs constraints and a field, both spatial and temporal,

through which players or inhabitants move. The project draws its premise from the notion of the singularity, as developed by theorists like Ray Kurzweil—the idea that accelerating technology will lead to the emergence of a demiurgic artificial intelligence, which will revolutionize all aspects of life. In *Ornament,* we forecast that this event will not only radically transform social interactions and cause global political change but also breed a range of competing realities, each of which is developed as a scenario in the computer game. Each of these realities is articulated through our design of the capabilities and attributes of the player, the spaces with which the player interacts, and the rules of the game. Every player has the ability to chart a path across possible futures, altering his or her own destiny as well as the destinies of thousands of other players. In the *Ornament* world, computation is cheap, pervasive, and distributed, catalyzing the emergence of a massive, global lower-middle class and giving rise to an ecology of superfast portable devices powered by hydrogen cells, steam-tech windups, flywheel batteries, and bioelectrics. The game combines a role-playing environment in which social structures form and evolve among players with a first-person action game. Most important, players have channels for interacting not only with information but with the fabric of time itself. This idea potentially has radical implications for architecture: how might architects design environments that enable users to manipulate and shape their own surroundings? While situated in the realm of fiction, *Ornament* anticipates a near future in which the boundaries between the virtual and the

urban game have been confused, blurred, or even erased, asking what "play"—and freedom—might be in the twenty-first century.

1. Henri Bergson, *Creative Evolution* (1911; New York: Modern Library, 1944), 20.

In the late nineteenth and early twentieth centuries, photography and film revolution-ized the way people saw the world. Previously imperceptible details were captured; the movements of human, animal, and technological bodies could be recorded; whole new realities could be fabricated. Walter Benjamin famously argued that these technologies of mechanical reproduction would lead people to perceive architecture in a new way—what he called a "mode of distraction." The late twentieth century has seen an intense proliferation of new digital technologies that may give rise to their own modes of perception—not least the virtual realities of contemporary popular cul-ture. How will architecture respond to these changes? Will the rise of visual immer-sive technologies lead to a de-emphasis of real three-dimensional spaces, or will it instigate new modes of experiencing and designing spaces?

Mark Wigley frames the issue of electronics and perception within the contemporary political landscape, suggesting that in a world predicated on movement and flows, the power of architecture may be its ability to give pause. Anthony Vidler offers a psy-choanalytic parable in four scenes—featuring progressively more advanced screens—to describe the transformation of the twentieth-century architectural subject.

Several architects actively working with new digital technologies provide examples of how architecture might incorporate or respond to electronic modes of perception. Elizabeth Diller presents two recent projects produced in collaboration with Ricardo Scofidio, including an unrealized media project that would have used electronic technologies to generate new kinds of social interactions within an intentionally low-resolution environment.

Nigel Coates also explores the spatial ramifications of new media. His film *Ecstacity* follows six inhabitants of a semifictional city inundated by electronic and cultural flows, suggesting ways to inhabit the new global metropolis. Hani Rashid and Lise Anne Couture discuss the impact of the computer on their practice and the way that the experience of their Hydra-Pier pavilion is affected by digitally influenced modes of perception.

Finally, Frederic Levrat and Sulan Kolatan offer two perspectives on the impact of electronic technologies on different kinds of interfaces. In Levrat's case, architecture becomes an interface between the visual realm of information saturation and the physical realm of individual experience; in Kolatan's formulation, digital technologies give rise, particularly in their emphasis on the sensory rather than the merely visual, to the confusion of boundaries between bodies, spaces, and technologies.

Mark Wigley

Still Effects

Addressing electronics and perception during war-time, it would be all too easy to lapse into generic statements about the increasingly electronic means of killing people and the electronic ways that we now watch the killing in real time. But I think it is better to talk about war before it happens rather than during it, when even the most critical discussions tend to become unconsciously aligned with the rhythms and mentality of network television, adjuncts to the very forces being criticized. Instead of tuning in to the issue at the same time as everyone else, architects need to be tuned in all the time and to constantly confront the difficult questions of architecture's relationship to war, violence, terrorism, power, and so on—cultivating a new sense of responsibility for our discipline.

Inside the university, we address these issues within the unique context of a very old institution that promotes reflection, analysis, discussion, experimentation, and above all, hesitation. Hesitation—the idea that one can step outside of a situation, carefully reflect on it, and then reenter armed with new insights and possibilities for action—is the exceptional gift of the university.

As architects, we know something about hesitation—that moment of unexpected pleasure or mystery that a building can produce. Isn't it this hesitation that unites us, despite our very different ideas about what architecture is or should be? Perhaps architects can make a special contribution to the reflection going on within the university and beyond by provoking in others the kind of hesitation that we experience in the face of the buildings we love. Architects are public intellectuals, cultivating reflection about the world in the world. We are engaged in a field that is always at once cerebral and practical, ideal and material, and inside and outside of the university. Our greatest responsibility is to collaborate and to exploit all our resources— drawings, models, buildings, exhibitions, books, films, web sites, and so on—to produce thoughtful hesitation in the community we serve.

A few quick observations about electronics and perception. First, perception itself is electronic. Just look inside your head: neurons firing away. Second, less and less do we perceive things without electronic aids. Third, you cannot see electronics, only its effects. This is a complex topic, then, but as architects we are experts on the relationship between the visible and invisible, so we have much to say about electronics.

The twentieth century was the age of electronics, beginning in 1897 with the identification of the electron and in 1905 with its first practical application in the form of the diode valve. Initially, architects saw—perhaps too clearly—electronics as separate from architecture. In its default setting, architecture is the production of the effect of stillness, an amazing effect in a world that is endlessly moving. And since electronics is nothing but movement, the controlled movement of a negative charge, our default reaction was to see electronics as separate from architecture, as either being housed by architecture or extending it. This was the case at the beginning of the century. By the end, however, we were in the opposite situation: seeing—again too clearly—architecture inside electronic flows. Perhaps what we have found within these flows are new forms of stillness, new forms of our old magic. Perhaps we have yet to expose ourselves to the risks of movement that we have celebrated so long and so loudly. At the beginning of the twenty-first century, after one hundred years of thinking about and reacting to electronics, I wonder if architects are really ready to act differently, to think differently.

Anthony Vidler

Screened Identities

What kind of subject is constructed through the use of the digital tools that today produce such entrancing surfaces? Jacques Lacan offers us a way of thinking about this question, for it was he who taught us that in gazing at a screen, a split occurs between being and semblance. This split forms during what Lacan calls the mirror stage: the fabled moment when the six-month-old infant is held up by its mother in front of the mirror and recognizes an image that (unhappily) is not its mother but itself—scaled down in size, reversed, and mute, a self as a picture, forever separated from the physical being that knows itself only through this image and will forever in vain try to "join" itself with this image; hence paranoia, neurosis, schizophrenia.

In following through with the implications of Lacan's analysis, we might consider the nature of this mirror stage in its successive historical contexts, such that each moment of modernism has a corresponding mirror or screen and constitutes its own special kind of subject. So let me briefly rewrite the architectural history of modernism as a short story, the story of the babes in the mirrors.

My first modern mirror stage is set in late-nineteenth-century Vienna: our baby architect is surely held in the prosthesis designed by Daniel Gottlieb Moritz Schreber (father of Freud's Schreber), inventor of mechanical aids for child deportment as terrifying as the writing machine in Kafka's "Penal Colony." The mirror is full-length, spotted, and framed ornately in gilt wood carved in the writhing shapes of pre—Art Nouveau soft-porn nymphs and satyrs. The combination of the iron frame enclosing our baby designer, the shadow of a nanny hovering in the background, and the animated eroticism of the mirror frame might produce a specific type of alienated subject, one filled with vague neurasthenia, riven with the mutual anxi-eties of agoraphobia and claustro-phobia, and doomed to live in Jugendstil interiors that are, to use Benjamin's terms, as sterile as the electric wiring twining around their coldly sexual decoration.

The adult form of this baby might be Adolf Loos, living like Kafka in a Chinese puzzle land of little boxes, each one for a specific purpose, of a different scale, and incorporated into the next in a totalizing game of what Loos called three-dimensional chess—the game of the *Raumplan.* Outside the puzzle, however, in the new public realm, our subject is dressed, Max Weber–style, without charisma, in gray overcoat, black tie, and homburg hat, ready for the office and really cool.

My second scene takes up the Lacanian subject in the 1930s. Our child architect is held up in a French *trotte-bébé,* or baby walker; replacing nanny, a modern mother is now at hand, her face perhaps merging with the outlines of the baby's own reflection, while the room would be white, of ambiguous spatial dimensions, and sparsely furnished. The mirror emphasizes the transparency of glass—the glass house in which Breton dreamed and the glass house that Mies van der Rohe built. Its frame is chrome, perhaps designed in a circular form by Eileen Gray, with a little enlarging glass extending from its center so that the reflection is distorted and reversed twice over, as if depicted by Braque or, maybe worse, Picasso.

The socialized subject that develops from this baby might itself be divided. On the one hand, it has the desires of a surrealist like Matta, with his dreams of a soft, womblike house. On the other hand, it harbors the modernist drive toward spatial power—epitomized by Ayn Rand, who we might imagine cross-dressed as Cary Grant in the role of Howard Roark, supremely confident of overcoming the insufferable alienation of a tactile-phobic, anti-city, anti-crowd, anti-woman world by a gesture toward the "über-architektur" of the skyscraper. Our baby might grow up to build a glass house for itself in Connecticut and remain trapped for the rest of its life between modernism and postmodernism.

My third baby is more tentative in its construction, the product of an era characterized at once by refusal—a refusal of reflection, of transparency, of extension—and by resignation—a resignation that the grand narratives of introjection and projection that characterized historicist and modernist space-time models no longer hold. It is a space of absolute self-consciousness of prehistory and posthistory, as if the baby architect, now held firmly by a dedicated caregiver of any age and gender, knows all the tricks. It is somehow aware, as the psychoanalyst Sami-Ali has proposed, that in looking at itself and being denied its desire to capture the face of the mother, it is committed to a split identity, not only between imago and I, ego, but between two imagos, so to speak, blurred into a distorted physiognomy that is far from transparent, rather opaque and translucent. This subject is truly "lost in space" (cf. Mark Wigley), wandering vaguely in a state of continuous psychasthenia and ready to be devoured by the very object of its fear.

The imago of this subject is scanned and projected back not as reflection but as television screen. This subject might grow up to become something between a paranoid theorist obsessed with codes, whether in football or form, and a wild expressionist defending himself against the void by ever more contorted shapes. In architectural terms, it would be situated somewhere in the space between Peter Eisenman and Frank Gehry.

But what of our new baby, one not yet decided to be an architect but destined to play out this role on the stage of the twenty-first century? It

would be one graduating from hours of Teletubbies to Playstation 2, one who at the age of fifteen plays "SOCOM: The U.S. Navy Seals," intently counting up its kills and deaths while CNN plays the real war on television. The mirror now would be digital, not analog, and subject to endless morphing (cf. Karl Chu), while the picture in the mirror assumes the form of a hyperreal three-dimensional image or even a holographic lasergram. The mirror now resembles William Gibson's grayed-out, neuromantic computer screen; it exists in a matrix where introjection and projection are merged in a timeless state of warped and intersecting planes: what Gibson calls "a three-dimensional chessboard extending to infinity." It is a matrix where no imago of the alienated self can be captured, where the subject, if indeed it can be called one, is self-identified only in the mind, jacked into the half-mental, half-software worlds of abandoned web sites and omnipotent IP controllers.

The socialized version of this subject would be found in the arcade of the Westfield Mall in Connecticut, playing "Area 51" with a red plastic gun. Later, as an architect, it will reproduce its own DNA in spatial terms, but now it will occupy a space that can be experienced only through mental sensation, where the visual has finally been entirely absorbed into a supersensory synthesis of all five traditional senses. Indeed, there is no need to stray far from the digital instruments that induce the sensation of "architecture"—those embedded biochips that the new monopoly called NanoSoft has made ubiquitous—and that allow us, the nomads of flow, to take our constructions, along with everyone else's, wherever we go.

It is only later in life, through the bioministrations of a nano-psychiatrist, that this subject will recognize that its primal scene took place one sunny day by a lake in Switzerland,

when dressed to kill in a "braincoat" it was plunged suddenly into a cloud, where, in a moment, all fixed position, all fixed identity, all high resolution have become no more than a blur (cf. Diller + Scofidio). It was at this point that the subject of visual electronic technology became blind.

LIVENESS AND MEDIATION

Elizabeth Diller

Within broadcasting, airing an event "live"—that is, at the precise moment of its occurrence—may be the last stronghold of auratic experience. Liveness turns a passive viewer into an eyewitness. It holds the titillation of the uncut, uncensored, and not fully controlled. Live is unmediated and immediate, as opposed to mediated, a word that implies distorted, doctored, inauthentic, and other bad things. Yet as we lose ourselves in the live images fed from journalists "embedded" abroad, we know that a producer and director in a control room somewhere are deciding what to air and what not to air, where to clip and where not to clip. In other words, we know that live entails a great deal of mediation.

This relationship between liveness and mediation has been an obsession in our work. For instance, we are currently designing a public artwork called *Facsimile,* in which an LED screen twenty-seven feet wide and sixteen feet high travels on a horizontal track along the facade of the Moscone Convention Center in San Francisco, broadcasting live video feed from several cameras pointed into the building. The images present a mix of fact and fiction, as prerecorded vignettes are intermittently substituted in place of the live footage. The viewer can never be sure whether the video images are real or staged.

Another recent project in which we explore the issue of liveness and fidelity is the Blur Building, a temporary pavilion designed for the Swiss Expo 2002. World's fairs and national expos are typically competition grounds for state-of-the-art technologies, multimedia spectacles, and simulation extravaganzas. These large-scale exhibitions feed the public's insatiable appetite for images of greater and greater technological virtuosity. The key word is immersive. In visual and acoustic delivery systems, success is based on how closely the systems simulate the real. Satisfaction is measured in pixels per inch. By contrast, Blur is decidedly low-definition. Its primary building material is one indigenous to the site: water. Water is pumped from the lake, filtered, and shot as a fine mist through a dense array of high-pressure nozzles, creating a constantly shifting fog mass. Blur challenges the orthodoxy of high resolution by presenting a formless, featureless, scaleless, depthless, spaceless, massless, and surfaceless space. Upon entering the fog mass, visual and acoustic references are erased, leaving only an optical whiteout and the white noise of pulsing fog nozzles.

The visitor in Blur is deprived of vision, the master sense that guides our navigation of the physical environment and social relations and that we use to assess identity, gender, age, race, and social status. Thus, for the media component of the project, which unfortunately was never realized, we collaborated with Ben Rubin to design a compensatory social communications system that would extend the body's natural system of perception. We were curious whether wireless communications systems, which typically rely on written and spoken language, could acquire more intelligence and a greater communicative power to transmit emotions and expressions of personal attraction, aversion, or embarrassment. We became interested in supplementary communications like involuntary responses—particularly the blush.

The project introduces a proxy telecommunications network recalibrated to a human scale that enhances communication within the mass of the fog. A prosthetic skin in the form of a raincoat equipped with a "sixth sense" allows visitors to navigate the fog mass and to interact with each other without speaking. Visitors enter a log-in station and fill out a questionnaire. Answers to this questionnaire are used to produce a response profile for each visitor that is added to a database. Each visitor is also given a "braincoat," a smart raincoat with embedded technologies that includes an imprint of the visitor's response profile, enabling the coats to communicate with one another inside the structure.

The basis for this communication is the cumulative database, a multidimensional statistical matrix that comprises a kind of data cloud parallel to the fog. When two people with a high level of affinity approach each other, the coats glow a warm color; when they have a high level of antipathy, they emit a green hue. There are other kinds of responses as well, including a possible acoustic signal emanating from a speaker embedded within the coat. Finally, if two people with 100 percent affinity encounter each other, there is a tactile response: small pads in the rear pockets of the braincoat vibrate, mimicking the tingle of excitement that comes with real physical attraction.

Blur Building, Lake Neuchâtel, Switzerland, 2002

Architects who work with computers typically conceive forms in the abstract and then transfer them into the world. I want to reverse the process and use the city as we perceive it as my starting point. This is the essential idea behind *Ecstacity,* a film I created for a recent architecture show in Graz called "Latent Utopias." In the film, it's not the buildings that are important but the total flow of the city. The film's six narrators reflect on the process of getting to know a city and making what one wants out of it. *Ecstacity* is not meant to be a manifesto for an electronic way of living. Rather, it portrays a city where experience is a combination of the ordinary and the extraordinary.

Welcome to one of the great cities of the world. Ecstacity is here and everywhere, a place where people and cultures meet. It blends everyday qualities drawn from Tokyo, Cairo, London, New York, Rome, Mumbai, and Rio de Janeiro into an urban kaleidoscope marked by cultural infusion. Despite its proliferation of lifestyles and global communication, Ecstacity puts emotion first. It is utopian insofar as it exists in the mind. Experiences are its bricks and mortar.

ECSTACITY

TUNING IN
You're taking off for Ecstacity. Postcards of it flash in your mind: images of Big Ben, the Body-plex, and the Ecstaloop, the symbol of the city. You've heard it's both clear and complex, with an ethereal, dynamic sort of architecture.

LOCKING ON
Seven zones blend seven cultures. Together they make one city that thrives on diversity and tolerance. Visceral new buildings add to traditional monuments. They simultaneously concentrate events and energize their surroundings.

UNDRESSING
The body is at the root of Ecstacity's feel for space—not some idealized body, but yours and mine. Invisibly, your body carries its own initial architecture with it, challenging and matching the world you are part of. It's our most intimate space.

LETTING GO
The Ecstaloop acts as a sign for the flaneur's meandering paths. Feel free to get lost and to build your own experiences out of the chaos of the place, from its complex spaces of streets and alleys to its cacophony of media options.

CRANKING UP
Local lifestyles flourish in the outer-urbs of Ecstacity. Here sensations and construction begin to join up, and built situations ebb and flow along with the desires that underwrite them. Vibrant hybrids diminish the brand domination of the suburbs.

FLIPPING OUT
An inversion of scale and sequence puts the city in your heart and in your head. Conversely, the city itself depends on the lives that inhabit it. Flipping and compressing extremes of intensity, the mental and the physical become each other's reality.

Real Virtuality

Hani Rashid / Lise Anne Couture

When we first acquired a computer, around 1992, we weren't quite sure what to do with it. It was too slow and mute to do much. At first it only seemed useful for flattening drawings—an expensive paperweight. Our initial idea was to utilize computing to make fly-through animations or to otherwise illustrate our designs. Once we saw some of the potentials, we realized that creating a fly-through was the last thing we wanted to do. At that point, the computer became a powerful tool for us to extend various sets of issues that we were already exploring in predigital media, through video and film, for instance—mainly those issues related to understanding and experimenting with new aspects of space and architecture. We were asking how we could make architecture more interactive, less autonomous, and possibly dematerialized.

By 1997, we became involved in a number of projects centered on multimedia and interactive spatial environments, including the Virtual Trading Floor for the New York Stock Exchange and the Guggenheim Virtual Museum. These projects looked at semiotics and the way that meaning is embedded on and within fluid and transformable surfaces and forms. We were interested in how a blurring of real and virtual spaces might lead to new ways of inhabiting space and architecture.

Recently, we have extended our investigations by exploring similar ideas in a series of built works. In contrast to the prevailing trend in digital animation and architecture, which is to try to make the virtual look real, we are interested in how the real can be rendered virtual. For example, our Hydra-Pier, a pavilion recently constructed in Haarlemmermeer, the Netherlands, attempts to appear dematerialized, computer-generated, and liquid by virtue of the way that it is realized formally and tectonically. We drew on ideas pertaining to the virtual that go back as far as seventeenth-century waterworks, spectacles, and follies. In the case of the Hydra-Pier, the water running over the roof of the building is not a spectacle of the movement of water but a spectacle of the dematerialization of the building mass. The pavilion is situated along a major landing descent route for airplanes at Schiphol Airport; to the viewer flying over it, the metallic color as well as the depth and speed of the running water—painstakingly engineered with water experts to achieve the exact effects we wanted—all work to dissolve the building into its surroundings, into the polder.

This notion of dissolution and transformation differs from older ideas of collage or cubist painting and is more akin to simulation, virtualization, or the new digital camouflage skins that read and simulate their surroundings in order to disappear. Today, a postcognitive way of experiencing buildings is emerging or reemerging, influenced by the increasing use of digital technologies in architecture. To be inside the Hydra-Pier, with the liquid above reflected in the shadows on the ground, is to have a visceral experience that cannot be articulated verbally or read in a conventional linguistic or semiotic way. Many layers of liquefaction are at play in this building, dissolving boundaries between the real and the virtual, between the natural and the artificial.

Hydra-Pier, Haarlemmermeer, the Netherlands, 2002

ARCHITECTURE AS INTERFACE

Frederic Levrat

BLURRING PERCEPTUAL BOUNDARIES

Sulan Kolatan

Perhaps more than any other site in the world, New York's Times Square embodies the challenge to architects posed by contemporary media. Nearly every surface penetrable by the eye (and rentable by the dollar) is covered with illuminated advertisements, running tickers, and LED screens featuring live video broadcasts. Here, the relationship between space and surface is pushed to its limits. Buildings become signs and signs become structures. Visual perception of surfaces supplants the other senses, including the tactile.

The proliferation of media produces effects of seamlessness and discontinuity at once. On one hand, it creates a self-referential and enclosed loop, as, for instance, Pokemon characters that originate on screen give rise to a franchise of physical objects—action figures, cards, and other accessories—that only acquire value from their association with the visual image. On the other hand, the media presents an inherent discontinuity, as images that originate in distant places reappear, or are re-materialized, elsewhere. At any given moment in Times Square, one can find images from far-flung places like Iraq, China, and Chicago collapsed and juxtaposed within a single space.

If we consider Times Square to be a symptom of larger trends rather than an anomaly, what does this signify for the future of architecture? Is there any role left for buildings—real, three-dimensional, physical spaces—in this world of ubiquitous media images and surfaces? How can architecture address the conditions of seamlessness and continuity presented by the media?

Architects must adapt by enlarging their primary sphere of concern from the physical realm to the visual and the virtual. By virtual I mean that which is constituted in the mind—the social imaginary, the brand, the values—which media helps attach to the experience of our environment. Architects can reveal the interactions between these different but coexisting dimensions. We should produce spaces that perform as interfaces between users and their environments, questioning the relationships between individual experiences of space and dislocated surfaces of information.

According to Georges Canguilhem, "An anomaly or mutation is not in itself pathological. Both express other possible norms of life."[1] The normality or pathology of a feature is thus contingent on its viability in a particular environment. I propose that early-twenty-first-century technologies create similar boundary problems between initially separate, specific systems, namely between the human body and various electronic systems. This is due not only to immersive environments such as virtual reality but also to the totalizing effect of visual, aural, and other ambient technologies surrounding us. Our newfound capacity to "be there," in many places at once, as we are when we speak on the phone or search the Internet, constitutes a significant ontological shift.

The symbiosis of artifact and user and the process of technology becoming "transparent" produce boundary problems akin to the effects of proprioceptive disorders. In these cases, an individual loses the "natural" sensory comprehension of various bodily extremities and, by extension, the ability to interact with the world normally. Examples include the statistical link between car accidents and cellular phone use or the disorientation and nausea caused by virtual caves.

As we move from visual techniques of observation to haptic techniques of immersion, how are new intersystemic relations between bodies, space, and technology constituted? What is the nature of boundaries in such constructions? Is the precise delineation of boundary even important? What are the criteria of viability for new modes of spatial perception?

1. Georges Canguilhem, *The Normal and the Pathological* (New York: Zone Books, 1991), 144.

Stan Allen

Stan Allen is a founding principal of Field Operations and dean of the Princeton School of Architecture. His built work includes galleries, exhibition design, and single-family houses. He has also addressed a variety of large-scale urban contexts through competitions and research. His publications include *Points and Lines: Diagrams and Projects for the City* (1999) and *Practice: Architecture, Technique and Representation* (2000).

Wiel Arets

Wiel Arets established his architecture practice in 1984. He currently holds the Berlage Chair at the Technical University of Delft and is the director of the Berlage Institute Ph.D. program. He has also taught at the Architectural Association in London, Columbia University, the Cooper Union for the Advancement of Science and Art, the Amsterdam Academy of Architecture, the Rotterdam Academy of Architecture, and the Royal Danish Academy of Fine Arts.

Michael Bell

Michael Bell is an associate professor at Columbia University, where he is co-director of the core design studios and coordinator of the housing studio. He is the editor of *Slow Space* (1998) and the author of two forthcoming books, *16 Houses: Designing the Public's Private House* and a monograph. Bell established his own architecture firm in 1989.

Andrew Benjamin

Andrew Benjamin is professor of critical theory at Monash University in Melbourne and Chettle Professor of Architectural Theory at the University of Sydney. He is the author of numerous books, including *Art, Mimesis, and the Avant-Garde: Aspects of a Philosophy of Difference* (1991), *What Is Abstraction?* (1996), *Present Hope: Philosophy, Architecture, Judaism* (1997), and *Architectural Philosophy* (2000).

Irene Cheng

Irene Cheng is a designer and writer living in New York City. She received her architectural training at the Columbia Graduate School of Architecture, Planning and Preservation.

Karl Chu

Karl Chu teaches at Columbia University and is codirector of the Genetic Architecture Program at the Universitat Internacional de Catalunya in Barcelona. His current research addresses the development of a new theory of genetic architecture derived from the convergence of computation and biogenetics.

Nigel Coates

Nigel Coates is a professor at the Royal College of Art in London. In 1985, he cofounded Branson Coates Architecture, a firm with commissions that include shops, restaurants, museums, and exhibitions such as "Guide to Ecstacity." Coates has also won recognition for his furniture and glass designs.

Beatriz Colomina

Beatriz Colomina is an architectural historian and theorist who has written extensively on architecture and the modern institutions of representation, particularly print media, photography, advertising, film, and television. At Princeton University, she is a professor of architecture, founding director of the Media and Modernity program, and director of Graduate Studies. Her books include *Architecture-production* (1988), *Sexuality and Space* (1992), and *Privacy and Publicity: Modern Architecture as Mass Media* (1994).

James Corner

James Corner is chair of the Department of Architecture and Regional Planning at the University of Pennsylvania. He is a founding principal of Field Operations. His design projects have won numerous awards, including the Daimler-Chrysler Award for Design Innovation in 2000. He is coauthor of *Taking Measures across the American Landscape* (1996) and editor of *Recovering Landscape: Essays in Contemporary Landscape Architecture* (1999).

Lise Anne Couture

Lise Anne Couture cofounded Asymptote, with Hani Rashid, in 1988. The firm's recent projects include the Guggenheim Virtual Museum, the Virtual Trading Floor for the New York Stock Exchange, Hydra-Pier in the Netherlands, and a new line of office furniture for Knoll International. She has been a professor in the Department of Architecture at Parsons School of Design since 1990.

Yolande Daniels

Yolande Daniels is an assistant professor of architecture at Columbia University. She is a partner with Sunil Bald in the design collaborative SUMO. The firm's most recent projects include information kiosks for Tosai University in Togane, Japan, and the temporary Museum for African Art in New York City. In 2003, she was awarded a Rome Prize in architecture.

Odile Decq

Odile Decq practices architecture in France. Together with her partner Benoit Cornette, from 1985 to 1998 she won numerous design awards and commissions, including university buildings and social-housing projects. Decq's recent designs include the Nanterre motorway bridge and operations center, an expansion of the Museum of Contemporary Art in Rome, and furniture for the UNESCO Headquarters in Paris. She has taught at Columbia University, the Bartlett School of Architecture, Technical University in Vienna, and Ecole Spéciale d'Architecture in Paris.

Elizabeth Diller

Elizabeth Diller is a founding principal of Diller + Scofidio, an interdisciplinary studio that fuses architecture with the visual and performing arts. Current projects include the Institute of Contemporary Art in Boston, the new Museum of Art and Technology for Eyebeam in New York, and the redesign of Lincoln Center's public spaces, also in New York. Diller is a professor of architectural design at Princeton University.

Evan Douglis

Evan Douglis is an adjunct professor and the director of the architecture galleries at Columbia University. He has also taught at the Cooper Union for the Advancement of Science and Art, Pratt Institute, and Parsons School of Design. Douglis is the recipient of an Emerging Voices Prize from the Architectural League of New York and a NYFA Fellowship in architecture/environmental structures.

Peter Eisenman

Peter Eisenman is an architect and educator. He has designed a wide range of innovative projects, including large-scale housing and urban design schemes, facilities for educational institutions, and a series of private houses. He founded the Institute for Architecture and Urban Studies, an international think tank for architecture. Eisenman is the Irwin S. Chanin Distinguished Professor of Architecture at the Cooper Union for the Advancement of Science and Art and the Louis Kahn Professor of Architecture at Yale.

Colin Fournier

Colin Fournier is a professor of architecture and urbanism at University College London. He was an associate with Archigram Architects and was the master planner for major urban development projects in the Middle East. He is currently based in London and Austria, and working in partnership with Peter Cook on the design and construction of a new museum of modern art in Graz.

Kenneth Frampton

Kenneth Frampton trained as an architect at the Architectural Association in London. He has worked as an architect and an architectural historian and critic in England, Israel, and the United States. He is currently the Ware Professor of Architecture at Columbia University. His books include *Modern Architecture: A Critical History* (1980), *Modern Architecture and the Critical Present* (1980), *Studies in Tectonic Culture* (1995), *American Masterworks* (1995), *Le Corbusier* (2002), and *Labor, Work, and Architecture* (2002).

Frank Gehry

Frank Gehry established Frank O. Gehry & Associates in 1962. Since then, he has produced public and private buildings in America, Europe, and Asia. His firm's recent projects include the Fisher Performing Arts Center at Bard College in Annandale-on-Hudson, New York, the Walt Disney Concert Hall in Los Angeles, and the Experience Music Project in Seattle.

Christian Girard

Christian Girard is an architect and theoretician practicing in Paris. His current projects include housing programs and public facilities. He is a founding member of and a professor at the Ecole d'Architecture Paris-Malaquais.

Elizabeth Grosz

Elizabeth Grosz teaches in the Women's and Gender Studies Department at Rutgers University. She has published widely on architecture, feminism, and philosophy. Her most recent book is *Architecture from the Outside: Essays on Virtual and Real Space* (2001).

Zaha Hadid

Zaha Hadid is a London-based architect known for works such as the Vitra Fire Station and the Bergisel Ski Jump in Innsbruck, Austria. Her designs include pavilions, housing projects, and furniture. She has won numerous awards and competitions, including the Cardiff Bay Opera House in Wales and the BMW Central Plant Building in Leipzig, Germany. She has taught at the Architectural Association in London, the University of Chicago, Harvard, Columbia, and Yale Universities, and the University of Applied Arts, Vienna.

Laurie Hawkinson

Laurie Hawkinson is an architect and principal in the office of Smith-Miller + Hawkinson. The firm's recent projects include the Corning Museum of Glass in Corning, New York, and the North Carolina Museum of Art in Raleigh, North Carolina (in collaboration with artist Barbara Kruger and landscape artist Nicholas Quennell). She is currently an assistant professor of architecture at Columbia University.

K. Michael Hays

K. Michael Hays is the Eliot Noyes Professor of Architectural Theory at Harvard University and adjunct curator of architecture at the Whitney Museum of American Art. His books include *Modernism and the Posthumanist Subject: The Architecture of Hannes Meyer and Ludwig Hilberseimer* (1992), *Hejduk's Chronotype* (1996), and *Architecture Theory since 1968* (1998).

Steven Holl

Steven Holl established Steven Holl Architects in New York in 1976. Among his most recent honors are Progressive Architecture Awards for the Nelson-Atkins Museum of Art and the MIT Undergraduate Residence, a New York AIA Design Award for the Cranbrook Institute of Science in Bloomfield Hills, Michigan, and a National AIA Design Award for Kiasma, the Museum of Contemporary Art in Helsinki. Holl has taught at Columbia University since 1981.

Catherine Ingraham

Catherine Ingraham is chair of the Graduate Architecture and Urban Design program at the Pratt Institute. She has published and lectured widely on architecture and architectural theory. Her books include *Architecture and the Burdens of Linearity* (1998) and *The Discipline of the Milieu: Architecture and Post-Animal Life* (forthcoming). Ingraham has taught at Harvard and Columbia Universities, the University of Illinois at Chicago, and Iowa State University.

Ed Keller

Ed Keller is a designer, writer, architect, musician, and multimedia artist based in New York City. He is an adjunct assistant professor of architecture at Columbia University. In 1998, he founded Atelier Chronotype, a design research studio. The firm's current projects include an online game, screenplay, and sound installation. His research and essays have been published in *Architecture, Precis, Wired*, and *Metropolis.*

Jeffrey Kipnis

Jeffrey Kipnis is the curator of architecture and design at the Wexner Center for the Arts and a professor of architecture at Ohio State University. He has written *In the Manor of Nietzsche* (1990), *Philip Johnson: The Glass House* (1993), *Chora L Works: Jacques Derrida and Peter Eisenman* (1997), and *Perfect Acts of Architecture* (2001).

Sulan Kolatan

Sulan Kolatan has taught at Columbia University since 1990. She is a founder and principal of Kolatan/MacDonald Studio in New York City, a firm known for innovation in form and structure. Born in Istanbul, she studied at Rheinisch-Westfalische Technische Hochschule in Aachen, Germany, and Columbia University.

Rem Koolhaas

Rem Koolhaas founded the Office for Metropolitan Architecture in 1975 with Elia and Zoe Zenghelis and Madelon Vriesendorp. His books include *Delirious New York* (1978), *S,M,L,XL* (1995), *Mutations* (2001), and *Harvard Design School Guide to Shopping* (2002). He is a professor in practice of architecture and urban design at Harvard University.

Sanford Kwinter

Sanford Kwinter is a New York–based writer and a cofounder of Zone Books. He is an associate professor at Rice University and is currently teaching at the Harvard Graduate School of Design. His books include *Incorporations* (1992) and *Architectures of Time: Toward a Theory of the Event in Modernist Culture* (2001).

Sylvia Lavin

Sylvia Lavin is chair of the Department of Architecture and Urban Design at the University of California at Los Angeles. She writes widely on architectural history, theory, and criticism and is the author of *Quatremère de Quincy and the Invention of a Modern Language of Architecture* (1990) and *From Architecture to Environment: Richard Neutra and the Postwar House* (forthcoming). She has taught at Harvard and Columbia Universities, the Berlage Institute, and the University of Applied Arts in Vienna.

Frederic Levrat

Frederic Levrat is a founder of ARX New York, a firm that explores the convergence of architectural and cultural issues. He has lectured in the United States, Europe, and Japan. Currently he teaches at Columbia University and the Pratt Institute.

Greg Lynn

Greg Lynn is the principal of Greg Lynn FORM in Los Angeles, a firm that special-izes in adapting technologies from the aeronautic, automobile, and film industries to create innovative architectural forms. His design projects include a social hous-ing project in Amsterdam, a coffee and tea set for Alessi, and a collaborative entry for the World Trade Center competition. He teaches at the University of California at Los Angeles, Columbia and Yale Universities, and the University of Applied Arts in Vienna.

Winy Maas

Winy Maas is a founding partner of the Rotterdam-based firm MVRDV. The office is known for provocative projects, such as Metacity/Datatown and Pig City, that address technology and sustainability. Maas has received numerous design awards and lectures widely. He has taught at Yale University, the Berlage Institute, the Architectural Association in London, and Technical University in Vienna.

Scott Marble

Scott Marble is a partner at Marble/Fairbanks Architects. He was a New York Foundation for the Arts Fellow in Architecture in 1994. He has taught at Columbia University since 1987 and has edited *Abstract,* the school's catalog of student work, since 1995. He coedited the book *Architecture and Body* (1998).

Reinhold Martin

Reinhold Martin is an assistant professor of architecture at Columbia University and a partner in the firm Martin/Baxi Architects. He is a founding editor of the journal *Grey Room.* His publications address the history and theory of postwar modern architecture and related subjects. He is coauthor, with Kadambari Baxi, of *Entropia* (2001) and author of *The Organizational Complex: Architecture, Media, and Corporate Space* (2003).

Thom Mayne

Thom Mayne is a founder of Morphosis, an award-winning firm based in Los Angeles. He was a founder of the Southern California Institute of Architecture and is currently a professor at the University of California at Los Angeles. He has also taught at Harvard, Columbia, and Yale Universities and the Berlage Institute.

Mary McLeod

Mary McLeod is an associate professor of architecture at Columbia University. Her research focuses on the history of the modern movement and contemporary theory, particularly the connection between architecture and ideology. She is coeditor of *Architecture, Criticism, Ideology* (1985) and *Architectureproduction* (1988), and has recently completed a book on the French designer Charlotte Perriand.

Detlef Mertins

Detlef Mertins is Canada Research Chair in Architecture at the University of Toronto. He was professional adviser for the Downsview Park Competition in Toronto. He has edited *Metropolitan Mutations: The Architecture of Emerging Public Spaces* (1987), *The Presence of Mies* (1994), and Walter Curt Behrendt's *The Victory of the New Building Style* (1999). He is currently completing a monograph on Mies van der Rohe and coediting an English translation of the avant-garde journal *G: Material for Elementary Form-Creation*.

Victoria Meyers

Victoria Meyers has taught architecture at Columbia University since 1993. She is a founding principal of Hanrahan/Meyers Architects. Her studies of light from natural and artificial sources have led to unique solutions in gallery and performance space designs, and are the subject of a forthcoming book.

Toshiko Mori

Toshiko Mori established an architecture practice in New York City in 1981. Her work combines architecture with art in projects ranging from houses and stores to museums and institutions. In her research and practice, she is interested in innovative materials and fabrication methods that draw on both new and traditional techniques. Her most recent book is *Immaterial/Ultramaterial* (2002). Mori is chair of the Department of Architecture at the Harvard Graduate School of Design.

Enrique Norten

Enrique Norten is a founder and principal of TEN Arquitectos, based in Mexico City and New York. He holds the Miller Chair at the University of Pennsylvania. He has won numerous design awards, including Latin American Building of the Year for his Hotel Habita in Mexico City. Recently, Norten won the competition to design the new Visual and Performing Arts Library in Brooklyn, New York.

Joan Ockman

Joan Ockman is an architecture critic and historian. She has taught at Columbia University since 1985 and directs the Temple Hoyne Buell Center for the Study of American Architecture. Among the books she has edited are *Architecture Culture 1943–1968: A Documentary Anthology* (1993), *The Pragmatist Imagination: Thinking about Things in the Making* (2000), and *Out of Ground Zero: Case Studies in Urban Reinvention* (2002).

Gregg Pasquarelli

Gregg Pasquarelli is a founding partner of SHoP and an adjunct assistant professor of architecture at Columbia University. The firm has won several design awards, including the 2001 Academy Award in Architecture from the American Academy of Arts and Letters. SHoP's recent projects include a residential tower in Brooklyn, a pedestrian bridge in lower Manhattan, and a residence in Aspen, Colorado.

Wolf Prix

Wolf Prix cofounded Coop Himmelb(l)au in 1968. The firm's projects include the Rooftop Remodeling in Vienna, the master plan for the city of Melun-Sénart in France, the Museum Pavilion in Groningen, the Netherlands, the UFA Cinema Center in Dresden, Germany, and the "Apartmentbuilding Gasometer B" in Vienna. He is dean of the University of Applied Arts in Vienna.

Mark Rakatansky

Mark Rakatansky is principal of Mark Rakatansky Studio. His designs and writings have appeared in a range of publications in Asia, Australia, Europe, and the United States. He teaches design and theory at Columbia University.

Hani Rashid

Hani Rashid is a cofounder, with Lise Anne Couture, of Asymptote, a practice specializing in architectural and interactive digital design. Projects include the Guggenheim Virtual Museum, the Virtual Trading Floor for the New York Stock Exchange, Hydra-Pier in the Netherlands, and a new line of office furniture for Knoll International. He has taught at Columbia since 1989 and has codeveloped the school's digital design studio program.

Jesse Reiser

Jesse Reiser is a founder and principal of Reiser + Umemoto RUR Architecture, an innovative and award-winning laboratory of architecture, urban infrastructure, and landscape architecture. Currently an assistant professor at Princeton University, he has lectured and taught throughout the United States and Europe. He was a fellow of the American Academy in Rome in 1985.

Terence Riley

Terence Riley is chief curator of the Department of Architecture and Design at the Museum of Modern Art in New York, where he organized the landmark retrospectives "Mies in Berlin" and "Frank Lloyd Wright: Architect." Before joining the museum, he established an architectural practice with John Keenan in New York City.

Yehuda Safran

Yehuda Safran teaches architecture and theory at Columbia University. He has written widely about architecture, curated numerous architecture exhibitions, and is the author of *Mies van der Rohe* (2001). Currently based in Paris and New York, Safran has taught in England, the Netherlands, and China.

Saskia Sassen

Saskia Sassen is the Ralph Lewis Professor of Sociology at the University of Chicago. She is the author, most recently, of *Globalization and Its Discontents* (1999) and *Global Networks, Linked Cities* (2002).

Michael Sorkin

Michael Sorkin is an architect, writer, and teacher based in New York City. His design practice is devoted to both practical and theoretical projects at all scales, with a special interest in the city. His recent projects include master planning in Hamburg and Schwerin, Germany, planning for a Palestinian capital in East Jerusalem, and studies of the Manhattan waterfront and Far Rockaway. His books include *Variations on a Theme Park* (1991), *Wiggle* (1998), *Some Assembly Required* (2001), and *The Next Jerusalem* (2003). He is director of the Graduate Urban Design Program at the City College of New York.

Lars Spuybroek

Lars Spuybroek is the principal of NOX, based in Rotterdam. His work focuses on the relationship between architecture, media, and computing. Recent projects include video and electronic artworks as well as an interactive tower for the Dutch city of Doetinchem; Son-O-House, "a house where sounds live"; and a complex of cultural buildings in Lille, France. He is a professor at the University of Kassel.

Robert A. M. Stern

Robert A. M. Stern is an architect, teacher, and writer. He is currently dean of the Yale School of Architecture and was previously professor of architecture, director of the Historic Preservation Program, and the first director of the Temple Hoyne Buell Center at Columbia University. He is the author of numerous books, including a multivolume series on the history of New York City.

Mark C. Taylor

Mark C. Taylor is the Cluett Professor of Humanities and Religion at Williams College. He has written extensively on philosophy, religion, art, architecture, media, science, and technology. He cofounded the Global Education Network, an Internet-based company that develops college-level courses in the humanities, liberal arts, social sciences, and sciences. In the fall of 2002, his first art exhibition, "Grave Matters," opened at the Massachusetts Museum of Contemporary Art.

Bernard Tschumi

Bernard Tschumi was dean of the Columbia Graduate School of Architecture, Planning and Preservation from 1988 to 2003. In 1983, he won the competition to design Parc de la Villette in Paris. He established his Paris office in 1983 and his New York office in 1988. His books include *Architecture and Disjunction* (1994), *Event-Cities* (1994), and *Event-Cities 2* (2000).

Nanako Umemoto

Naneko Umemoto is a founder and principal of Reiser + Umemoto RUR
Architecture. She studied at the Cooper Union for the Advancement of Science
and Art and the School of Design at the Osaka University of Art in Japan.

Anthony Vidler

Anthony Vidler is an architecture historian and dean of the Irwin S. Chanin School of
Architecture at the Cooper Union for the Advancement of Science and Art. He has
received awards from the Guggenheim Foundation and the National Endowment for
the Humanities and was a Getty Scholar at the Getty Research Institute. His books
include *The Writing of the Walls: Architectural Theory in the Late Enlightenment* (1987),
The Architectural Uncanny: Essays in the Modern Unhomely (1992), and *Warped
Space: Art, Architecture, and Anxiety in Modern Culture* (2000).

Mark Wigley

Mark Wigley is a professor of architecture and the director of advanced studios
at Columbia University. He is the author of numerous books and articles on architecture and contemporary theory, including *The Architecture of Deconstruction:
Derrida's Haunt* (1993), *White Walls, Designer Dresses: The Fashioning of Modern
Architecture* (1995), and *Constant's New Babylon: The Hyper-Architecture of Desire*
(1998). He recently coedited *The Activist Drawing: Retracing Situationist
Architectures from Constant's New Babylon to Beyond* (2001).

Gwendolyn Wright

Gwendolyn Wright is a professor of architecture at Columbia University and has
served as director of Columbia's Buell Center for the Study of American Architecture. She is the author of *Moralism and the Model Home: Domestic Architecture
and Cultural Conflict in Chicago, 1873–1913* (1980), *Building the Dream: A
Social History of Housing in America* (1981), and *The Politics of Design in French
Colonial Urbanism* (1991). She recently hosted *History Detectives,* a television
series for PBS.

Alejandro Zaera-Polo

Alejandro Zaera-Polo is the cofounder, with Farshid Moussavi, of Foreign Office Architects. The firm's projects include the Yokohama International Port Terminal in Japan and a collaborative proposal for the World Trade Center competition. Zaera-Polo has written for *El Croquis, A+U, Quaderns*, and *A.D.* He is currently dean of the Berlage Institute in the Netherlands.

ACKNOWLEDGMENTS   ILLUSTRATION CREDITS

We are grateful to the contributing authors for allowing us to publish their essays and images. Special thanks to Stephanie Salomon for attentive copy editing and to David Benjamin for meticulous editorial assistance. Andrea Monfried, Sasha Porter, and Evan Schoninger of The Monacelli Press provided guidance and help. Karen Hsu and Alice Chung of Omnivore contributed their immense talents to designing the book under rigorous time constraints. Last, thanks to Sonya Marshall and David Hinkle of the dean's office at the Columbia Graduate School of Architecture, Planning and Preservation for their ability to accomplish seemingly anything.
—B.T., I.C.